COMPETITIVE METHODS OF FORMING

COMPETITIVE METHODS OF FORMING

Proceedings of the conference on 'Competitive methods of forming', jointly sponsored by The Iron and Steel Institute and The Staffordshire Iron and Steel Institute, held at Bilston on October 15, 1970

The Iron and Steel Institute

ISI Publication 138
© *The Iron and Steel Institute, 1971*

All rights reserved

Price £1.75

ISBN 0 900497 27 0

 PRINTED BY Unwin Brothers Limited
THE GRESHAM PRESS OLD WOKING SURREY ENGLAND

Produced by 'Uneoprint'
A member of the Staples Printing Group   (UO9976)

Contents

FUTURE DEVELOPMENT IN POWDER METALLURGY

E. B. Farmer

HISTORY

Powder-metallurgy techniques were first used as long ago as 6 000 BC when iron
weapons and simple tools were produced. Iron oxides were reduced to spongy iron
in charcoal furnaces and hammered while hot by simple forging operations. The
most impressive part produced by this method was the Delhi Pillar dating from 300
AD, which weighs more than six tons. The Incas and their descendents also used
methods similar to those employed for producing hardmetals for making platinum
articles.

In 1921 the first patents for porous bearings were filed, and this, together with the
production of oil pump parts in the early 1930's, initiated today's powder parts
industry.

The growth of this industry has been quite spectacular, as shown in Fig. 1, which
shows the usage of iron powder in the USA since 1945. The powder parts industry
accounts for 60-70% of this usage. Over the last ten years the growth rate has
averaged 18% per annum. It is rather surprising that this has almost been achieved

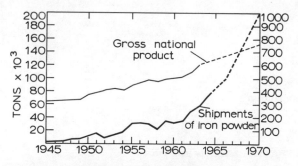

1 Total US shipments of iron powder

The growth of powder processes is noted, and shaping methods are compared with
alternative processes and future prospects, in terms of the advantages and disadvantages of the operations mentioned. Methods are classified according to the
degree and direction of pressure applied (which may be absent), and more detailed
indications of mechanisms and of the types of components produced by pressing,
impact forming, extrusion, rolling, and other methods of compaction are added. The
rolling, coining, isostatic pressing, and sinter-forging processes are regarded as the
most promising for future development. The properties of some products from the
author's company are assessed, and their uses indicated.

621.762.4.04

The author is Technical Director of Brico Engineering Ltd

by the use of one powder-shaping process, namely that of uniaxially cold pressing and sintering, with additional repressing and resintering together with infiltration where necessary. The bulk of the parts have also been made in relatively simple materials based on iron, copper, and carbon. There are a number of methods available for shaping metal powders in addition to conventional cold pressing (Table 1) but it is only in the last ten years that these processes have begun to be investigated in any great detail. Several of these have very great potential for increasing the scope and market penetration of powder metallurgy. Their introduction only depends on good process engineering.

Table 1 Methods of shaping metal powders

Pressure applied uniaxially	Pressure applied multiaxially	Shaping without pressure
Cold pressing	Isostatic and hydrostatic pressing	Loose shaping
Hot pressing		Slip casting
Hot coining	Explosive forming	Slurry casting
Sinter forging	Magnetic forming	Clay type moulding
Use of very high temperatures and pressures		High velocity projection
High energy rate forming		
Cold extrusion		
Hot extrusion		
Cold rolling		
Hot rolling		
Cyclic compaction		
Centrifugal compaction		

METHODS OF SHAPING METAL POWDERS

The major processing techniques available for shaping metal powders are given in Table 1, and can be divided into three groups.

Uniaxially applied pressure

COLD PRESSING

Usually mechanical presses have been used up to 1 MN (100 tonf) and above this range hydraulic presses. More recently mechanical presses of up to 5 MN (500 tonf) capacity have been employed. A typical hydraulic press of 1 MN (100 tonf) capacity is shown in Fig. 2 and a 2MN (200 tonf) mechanical press in Fig. 3. Using this technique, very close tolerances and compacts of intricate profile can be produced in the direction of pressing. Good surface finishes are obtained and there is little or no wastage of material. Production rates can be high. There are shape limitations,

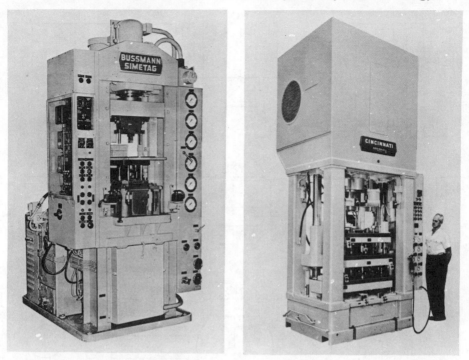

2 Typical 100 tonf hydraulic press   **3 200 tonf mechanical press**

however (Fig. 4). Generally tooling costs are high for complex parts and multi-cavity impressions and therefore long production runs are usually necessary, ideally 100 000 per annum or more, unless the piece part price is high.

In order to improve mechanical properties or produce parts of tighter tolerance, repressing and recoining, as well as additional sintering, are often used. Infiltration of a low density blank with copper or bronze has also been utilized to enhance mechanical properties or for applications where high hydraulic pressures have to be withstood.

HOT PRESSING

In order to eliminate the costly sintering operation, several types of press have been designed and manufactured to compact parts in a die and sinter them at the same time. A schematic cross-section of one type of hot press is shown in Fig. 5. The die in this case is graphite. Heating is supplied by a water-cooled high-frequency coil. A protective atmosphere can also be provided.

Very dense parts can be produced by this technique without the need for very high temperatures or long sintering times. Often lower pressing pressures can be used and better mechanical properties obtained with conventional materials, e.g. iron alloys, due to the high densities achieved. Powders difficult or impossible to press at room temperature, e.g. carbides, can be processed relatively easily by this technique. Figure 6 shows a typical press for producing cemented carbides.

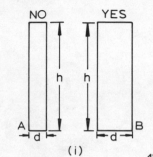

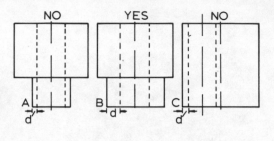

(i)

(ii)

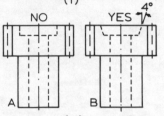

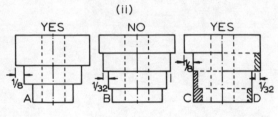

(iii)

(iv)

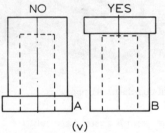

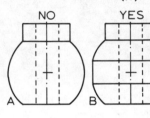

(v)

(vi)

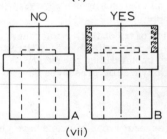

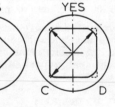

(vii)

(viii)

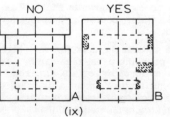

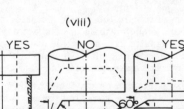

(ix)

(x)

(i) The ratio of h:d should not exceed 3:1, (ii) Avoid large and abrupt changes in cross-section. Such parts are difficult to compress to uniform density and tend to distort on sintering. The minimum wall thickness 'd' should exceed 1/32in (B). Off-centre hole giving thin wall should also be avoided (C), (iii) A short counter-bore can be formed with the top punch. A taper should be incorporated to facilitate removal of the tool (B), (iv) Parts with multiple steps (A) require concentric punches to achieve uniform density. Punch thickness should exceed 1/32in (B). Machining is reduced by moulding some of the steps. (C) Top flange exceeds 1/32in. (D) Narrow steps, (v) Blind holes are readily moulded, but if an external flange is also required it should be at the same end as the bottom of the blind hole, (B), (vi) Spherical sections can be moulded but a flat must be left on the o.d.(B) to avoid inadvertent contact between punches and feather edges to these. A land on the part (C) is even better. This can be moved on sizing. In plan also, feather edges (D) must be avoided (E), (vii) An external flange (A) is difficult and expensive to mould. A simple machining operation to provide such a flange (B) is preferable, (viii) Thin-walled sections (A) must be avoided (B). A uniform powder fill is difficult, density may vary and distortion occur on sintering. Radiusing the corners (C) facilitates die filling. A large concentric radius (D) simplifies machining of mating shaft, (ix) Re-entrant grooves and lateral holes cannot be pressed in the part (A). Simple machining after sintering can be used for such features (B), (x) Re-entrant tapers (A) cannot be moulded but must be machined in subsequently (B). Chamfers should not be less than 45° lest punch edges become fragile (C). A land (D) prolongs punch life

4 Some limitations of the cold-pressing process

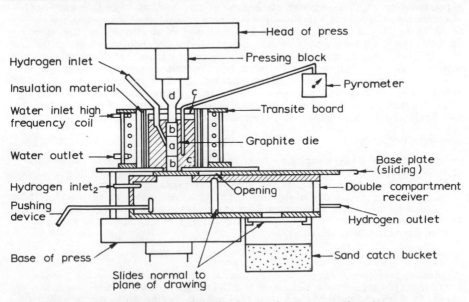

a *specimen;* b *carbide punches;* c *graphite cover;* d *spacer punch;* e *die*

5 Schematic cross-section through apparatus for hot-pressing iron compacts in a reducing atmosphere

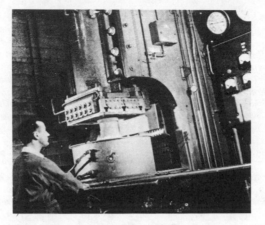

**6 Typical hot press for production of
cemented carbides**

The process is relatively slow, and compared with cold pressing, high capital outlay
is required for presses and heating equipment. Die wear can also be rapid and there
can be considerable difficulty in pressing and ejecting under a particular atmosphere.

A relatively new technique, spark sintering, can also be considered a development
of conventional hot pressing. Metal powders are simultaneously pressed and sintered but, unlike hot pressing, punches are employed as electrodes, and the powders
used to conduct high-density electrical energy of moderately high frequency (ac and
dc combined). A capacitor bank is used, mainly to tune the alternating current
superimposed on the direct current, but not for instantaneous power discharge.
Relatively low compacting pressures are needed. The process has been used for
producing exotic materials such as beryllium and titanium alloys, but at the present
stage of development the same major criticisms which are true of hot pressing are
also applicable to this technique. A typical layout is shown schematically in Fig. 7.

HOT COINING

During the last five years various efforts have been made to increase the density
of cold-pressed and sintered parts to obtain better mechanical properties or closer
tolerances. One such method is hot coining. After pressing and sintering, the part
is reheated and repressed in a conventional restrike or impact press. Considerable
densification takes place and therefore improvement in properties and tolerances.
While achieving its aim, the technique is expensive in that additional pressing and
heating equipment is required.

SINTER FORGING

In its most developed form the process consists of heating and sintering a blank
which in its hot state is placed in a forging press. The blanks or pre-forms are
simple in shape and most of the working takes place during the forging operation.
In this way up to 100% densification can be obtained as well as very close tolerances.
A typical part made by this technique is shown in Fig. 8 and a cross-section of the
case-hardened tooth form showing the high degree of densification in Fig. 9. The

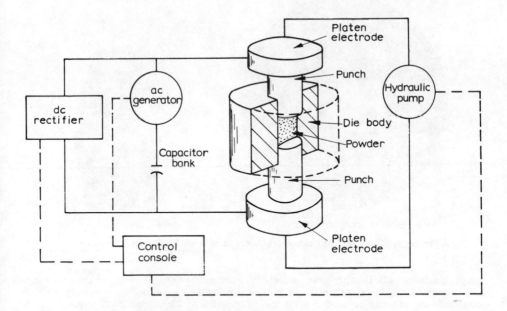

7 Schematic layout of spark sintering process

8 Pinion produced by sinter forging

photomicrograph (x200)   *case hardening pattern*

9 Microstructure and hardened tooth form of a sinter-forged pinion

major problem with this process is die life, particularly on complicated parts where
only about 20 000 parts are produced before a refacing operation is necessary. A
complete die set may be needed after the production of 70 000 or 80 000 parts.
Considerable attention was focused on the process when several cars of a well
known American manufacturer were fitted with sinter-forged con-rods.

USES OF VERY HIGH PRESSURES AND TEMPERATURES

By developing the work of Bridgeman at MIT a company in Sweden and one in the
USA, have, by using pressures of several thousand atmospheres and temperatures
in excess of 1 100°C, been able to produce large quantities of artificial diamonds.

HIGH-ENERGY RATE FORMING

A considerable amount of development work has been carried out on forming parts
by the Dynapak and other high-energy processes in order to produce maximum green
density. The process as developed at the moment is slow, however, and there is a
considerable problem with removing air from the compacts when very high pressures are applied in milliseconds. Pressed and sintered slugs have been successfully
formed by this method, particularly on the Petroforge machine, but as high a degree
of densification can be obtained by sinter forging.

COLD AND PASTE EXTRUSION

The main advantage of this process is that long thin objects can be made. For
example, with the paste process, pipes 500mm (20in) long, with diameters as low
as 1·5mm (0·060in) outside diameter and 0·7 (0·030in) internal diameter can be
produced. Materials which are difficult to shape can be manipulated by this process,
particularly hardmetal powders. Half-round, squared, twist drill, and tubular cross-
sections can be produced, as shown in Fig. 10. Since the material is in paste form

**10 Paste extrusion of various hardmetal powder
sections through shaped nozzles**

and does not have a high green strength until it is presintered or the binder removed,
difficulties in handling can occur. Sintered preforms can, of course, be produced
in the normal way and then extruded, either conventionally or isostatically. The main
advantage with this technique is that constant volume billets can be obtained and
unusual materials processed if isostatic extrusion is used. Little advantage has been
taken of this process in production to date.

HOT EXTRUSION

As with hot pressing this combines compacting and hot mechanical working to yield
a fully dense material. Controlled grain orientation and grain size can be obtained.
Good mechanical properties are also achievable.

It has found particular use in the atomic energy field for producing fuel elements by
using the canning technique, as is shown in Fig. 11. The material to be extruded is
placed in a stainless steel or some other suitable container and then extruded in
the conventional way, the penetrator method giving the best results. By using the
canning process, handling of toxic, pyrophoric, and radioactive materials can easily
be carried out and there is also no problem of providing a protective atmosphere
for conventional materials. The process is costly, however, and the canning material
has to be removed at the end of the operation. Particularly close tolerances cannot
be achieved and it can only be used to produce relatively simple shapes.

COLD ROLLING

Large quantities of thin copper and nickel strip are now produced by this technique.
Its advantages are that the capital cost of the plant is low (20% of the price of the
conventional plant for copper), as are production costs. The quality of the product

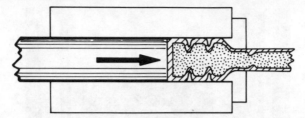

Folding metal can with loosely packed powders

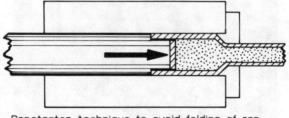

Penetrator technique to avoid folding of can

11 Canned extrusion of metal powders

is high and properties are uniform in all directions. Considerable difficulties result in trying to produce thick strip, for example, 1·52m (60in) diameter rolls are required to produce 0·5mm (0·02in) thick nickel strip. Usually the rolling speeds are much lower than conventional methods. An early powder roll feed arrangement is shown in Fig. 12.

Considerable interest has been stimulated recently by the work carried out by Bisra and Swansea University on the rolling of stainless steel and other alloy powders.

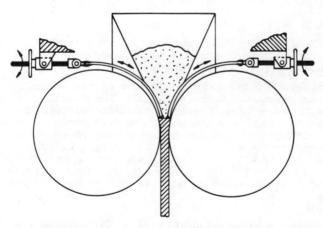

12 Schematic layout of an early powder roll feed arrangement after Franssen

HOT ROLLING

Using this approach, properties superior to cold-rolled strip can be obtained, but generally they do not approach the ultimate properties obtained by repeated cold rolling and sintering. Materials difficult to roll in a cold state, for example, tungsten- and molybdenum-based alloys, can be manipulated by this process. Although hot powders and/or hot rolls are used there is still a need to sinter the originally rolled strip to achieve maximum densification, and considerable difficulties are caused due to the need to use a protective atmosphere. A suggested sequence for the commercial production of strip is shown in Fig. 13.

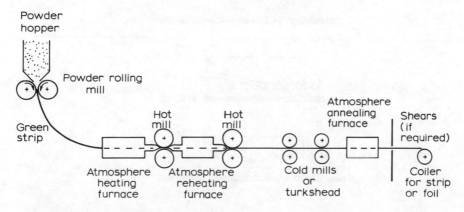

13 Suggested sequence for the commercial production of strip, sheet, and bus bar, by the powder rolling process

CYCLIC COMPACTION

The sequence of operations in continuous or cyclic compaction is shown in Fig. 14. In this technique a punch is continuously lowered and raised and the layer of powder on a suitable conveyor continuously advanced. Sections of considerable depth compared with powder rolling can be made. A variety of section shapes can be produced and the width of strip is only limited by the power of the press. The major limiting factor is the slow rate of production due to the reciprocating nature of the punch.

CENTRIFUGAL COMPACTION

In this process, powders mixed with a suitable binder are placed in a mould and spun to produce tubular or other symmetrical type components. The process is slow and difficulties can be encountered in obtaining a suitable binder. Stripping from the mould can also be a problem as can handling of the long cylindrical components. It has been used with some degree of success in isostatic compaction.

Pressure applied multiaxially

ISOSTATIC AND HYDROSTATIC PRESSING

Two main techniques are available, the wet bag, and the dry bag processes. With either technique better mechanical properties are obtained than with conventional

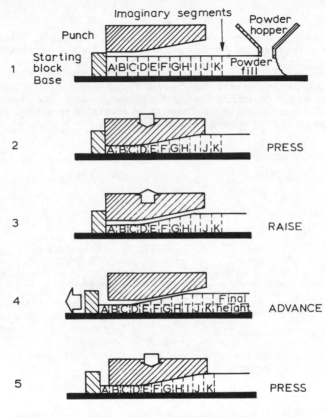

14 Operational sequence in cyclic compaction

die pressing. There is a uniformity of density in different sections, particularly on long components, and powders can be consolidated that are difficult or impossible to press by conventional cold pressing. Articles of complex shape can be compacted and no lubricants are necessary. Generally production rates are low. A simple schematic arrangement for compacting tungsten carbide powders is shown in Fig. 15. Pressure is applied to the fluid surrounding the rubber bag which then forces the steel tubes to compact the powder.

Currently high-speed isostatic presses are being developed for producing parts at rates as high as 48/min. These have been designed specifically for compacting ceramics, but with modifications could be successfully used for metal powders. The process would then have a very wide field of application.

EXPLOSIVE FORMING

Using this method, very high densities can be obtained. The powders undergo plastic rather than elastic deformation, the rate of forming being very high. Explosive form- ing has been used to produce rare and exotic alloys and those difficult to compact by any other process, but it is slow and cumbersome and the compact may disintegrate

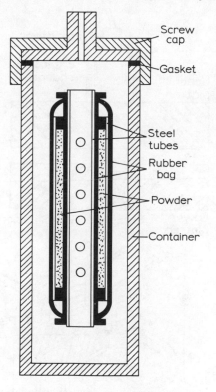

Screw
cap

Gasket

Steel
tubes

Rubber
bag

Powder

Container

**15 Isostatic pressure apparatus for
compacting tungsten carbide
powders**

on removal of the stress due to the tensile stresses set up being greater than the
dynamic fracture strengths of the material. Two designs of explosive press are
shown in Fig. 16.

MAGNETIC FORMING

Powders can be compacted by subjecting them to high pulsating magnetic fields.
This technique has only been used experimentally to date.

Shaping without pressure

LOOSE SHAPING

In this process powder is poured into a mould and then sintered. Limitations exist
as to the type of shape it is possible to obtain, but with ingenuity a wide range can be
produced. The method is simple to operate and the equipment cost is low. Theo-
retically there is no limitation on maximum permissible size, but this is governed
by the size of sintering furnace. The technique is mainly used for the manufacture

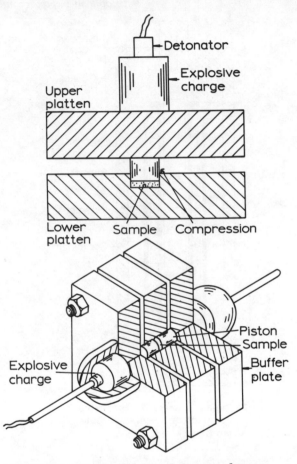

16 Explosive presses for compacting powders

of porous filters. The mould must be strong enough to contain the powders during sintering and usually graphite or cast iron is used. By choosing the correct powders, temperatures, and sintering time, dense parts of most metals and alloys can be obtained, but dimensional accuracy is poor. Typical filters are shown in Fig. 17.

SLIP CASTING

This method has been used for many years in the field of ceramics Tungsten, tantalum, and chromium were the first metal powders to be slip cast.

Slips consist of a suspension of particles, generally finer than 5 μm which are prevented from aggregating. This is controlled by adjusting the pH value. The slip, which is generally deflocculated before casting, is poured into a mould of plaster-of-Paris, which absorbs the liquid. The technique has been used for producing molybdenum crucibles (Fig. 18) and other parts. The principal stages of the process are shown in Fig. 19.

17 Sintered porous metal filters

18 Slip-cast molybdenum crucibles

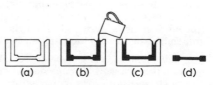

(a)   (b)   (c)   (d)

a *assembled mould;* **b** *filling the mould;*
c *absorbing water from the slip;*
d *finished piece removed from the
mould and trimmed*

**19 Principal stages of the slip-casting
    process**

SLURRY CASTING

This is similar to slip casting except that the metal is in the form of a slurry or cream which is poured into a mould and allowed to dry before extraction. Removal of the solvent can either be by slow evaporation or by absorption into the mould, usually made of plaster-of-Paris. Alternatively, solidifying liquid resins or other self-solidifying liquids can be used. The main disadvantage is the difficulty in obtaining slurries of sufficiently high density which can be poured, and which leave no residue on sintering.

The advantages of slip and slurry casting are that articles can be made in shapes and sizes not possible with conventional pressing and expensive equipment is not required. The processes work best with the finest powders, which are those most suitable for sintering. The dimensional accuracy is, however, poor, and the basic processes are slow. The technique is now being mechanized and very recently the author saw shapes being produced at a rate of 6 pieces/min.

CLAY-TYPE MOULDING

Although this method is well known in the ceramic industry, the moulding of clay-like metal masses without the use of pressure does not appear to have been seriously attempted, although the technique of spinning or sculpturing is an attractive one. To be a viable production proposition it would be necessary to avoid long drying out periods, and to obtain high densities with short sintering times. The main problem is in finding a suitable binder for the metal powder.

HIGH-VELOCITY PROJECTION

Gas or plasma spraying of powders has been used to deposit thin layers on to metal substrates, e.g. molybdenum or chromium on piston rings. The technique has also been used to produce parts of simple shape in materials which are very difficult to manipulate in any other way. It is unlikely that this will be used as a major parts manufacturing process in the future.

SHAPING PROCESSES WITH THE GREATEST POTENTIAL FOR DEVELOPMENT

Considerable shape limitations exist using conventional cold-pressing techniques (Fig. 4). In order to produce thin strip, powder rolling is being and will continue to be developed while the extrusion of powders will be exploited to produce continuous lengths of material of varying cross-sectional types. The primary products so produced will then be manipulated into parts by other shaping processes.

The development of high-speed isostatic pressing and automatic slip casting will open up new markets of considerable size which have previously been inaccessible due to shape limitations on pressing.

Hot coining and particuarly sinter forging, it is believed, have considerable potential because of the very close tolerances which can be produced, as well as properties similar to forged parts. This means that powder parts will be technically acceptable in the very high strength component field for the first time.

BRICO'S POSITION IN THE POWDER PARTS INDUSTRY

The average growth rate of the metal-powder parts industry in the UK has varied between 12 and 15% per annum over the last seven years. In the USA it has increased at a more rapid rate, 18% per annum.

By developing the methods of shaping metal powders, coupled with material development, it is believed that this growth rate can be increased considerably. This has been proved by experience at Brico, where, by using specially developed pressing and processing techniques as well as specially developed materials, a growth rate considerably in excess of the UK and USA national average has been achieved over the last five years (Fig. 20). For example, by developing special processes capable of producing piston rings at rates of up to 300/min a very large proportion of the UK European and USA market for small rings for all applications has been obtained, and as far as is known, Brico is the only producer of such components in volume production in the Western world.

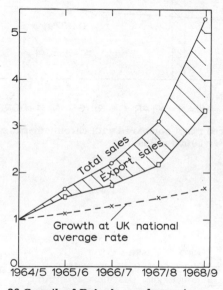

20 Growth of Brico's powder metallurgy unit, and the national average for powder metal parts with reference to 1964/65 level

Without the accompanying material development, however, this achievement would not have been possible. Figure 21 shows the wear properties of Brico Alloy 307 sintered automotive rings compared with chromium-plated and cast-iron rings, after extensive engine running. Under such operating conditions standard sintered materials would not perform as well as cast iron. The material developed also has a better scuffing resistance than chromium plate or cast iron and its mechanical properties are also at least as good as conventional-type materials (Fig. 22).

Valve seat inserts have to function under very arduous temperature and corrosion conditions and also have to withstand valve hammering. Sintered parts would not normally be considered for this application because of the quality requirements, but, as Fig. 23 shows, materials have been developed at Brico which can compete with all the best known conventional alloys. Without the use of sophisticated methods of shaping powders, however, the products would not be commercially viable. They

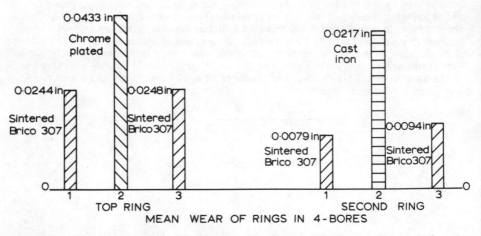

21 Wear of Brico sintered rings compared with chromium-plated top rings and cast-iron second rings after 50 000 miles

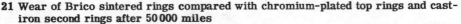

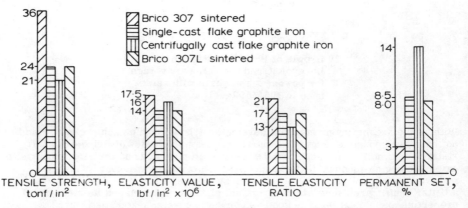

22 Typical mechanical properties of 3·250in diameter sintered, and conventional rings

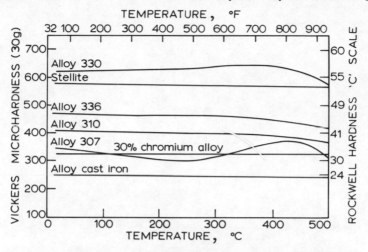

23 Effect of temperature of hardness of Brico sintered valve seat inserts compared with conventional valve seat materials

are currently being used in the heavy-duty diesel field, high-speed petrol engines, and also arduous air-cooled engine applications.

Brico has geared the powder-metallurgy unit to the production of parts with a high technological content, and by planned process, material, and product development aims both to keep its acknowledged position as an international leader in the field of powder metallurgy, and to maintain its current high growth and direct export rates, the latter of which amounted to 37% of total sales in 1968/69.

SCOPE OF COLD FORGING

D. J. Thornton

Cold forging can be defined as the forming of metal at ambient temperatures by force between a punch and die. Plastic flow of the material causes it to assume the shape of the tooling and so produce the required forging.

The development of the cold forging technique in this country has been due to the requirements of industry for a product with the strength and reliability of the traditional hot-forged component without their inherent disadvantages of forging scale, material decarburization, die wear dimensional variation, die mismatch, and draft angles giving large machining allowances.

Since its commercial introduction in the late 1950s, cold forging has grown to about 4% of the total UK forging production, and can be expected to increase in the future.

The adoption of this new process has been more rapid in the automotive industry than in industry generally. The modern four-cylinder car contains, in addition to the cold-headed fasteners, and nuts and bolts, over fifty individual cold-forged components ranging from a few grams to several kilograms in weight. This volume of parts could increase by 50% within the next few years.

To indicate the current development of the industry it is necessary to describe the basic process, typical manufacturing sequences for a cold-forged component, the range of materials suitable for the process, the types of parts currently produced, and the plant used in their production.

BASIC PROCESS

The process of cold forging consists of forming a material by pressure between a punch and die system. The three main types of cold forging, and their optimum proportions at maximum material deformation in a single operation are shown in Fig. 1; they are:

(i) the reverse extruded forging (can type), in which the material flows in the reverse direction to punch travel

(ii) the forward extruded forging (shaft type), in which the material flows in the same direction as punch travel

(iii) the headed or upset forging (flange type), in which the material flows at right-angles to punch travel.

The paper deals with the current state of the cold-forging technique in the UK. The rate of adoption of the process by industry is discussed together with the advantages of the process, possible applications, materials currently used, and tolerances commercially attainable. Manufacturing methods and tooling used to produce three typical components are described, with the process plant available for their production. The most economic applications for the use of this technique are given, with the areas of possible future development.

The author is with Ford of Europe Inc.

621. 777. 2/. 4. 016. 3

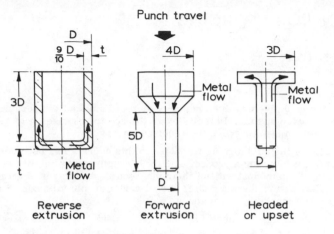

1 Basic types of cold forging

Cold drawing is also used as a finishing operation to produce thin wall tubes from reverse extruded cans.

Any or all of the three types of forging operations can be combined into an individual forging, and all three operations can be carried out simultaneously on some designs. The first two types can be considered as true extrusion operations as the forces applied to the slug are compressive, and it is in these operations that the maximum amount of material deformation is possible.

Because all the work is carried out at room temperature the pressures needed to overcome the material's resistance to plastic flow are high, up to 20 tonf/cm^2 for some steels. When deformation is taking place the material can be considered to be acting as a fluid submitting the tooling to equal loads in all directions. While most of the tooling is in compression and able to withstand the loads, the dies are in tension and it is necessary to support them with rings to combat the working pressure.

Most cold-forged parts are symmetrical about their axis and regular in section, being round, square, or hexagonal, and to avoid tooling failures the simplest possible shape should be specified compatible with component design requirements.

In order to prevent metal-to-metal contact between the cold forging and the tooling, the raw material is coated with a lubricant; in the case of steel this usually takes the form of zinc phosphate followed by a stearate soap. This two-part treatment in which the zinc phosphate forms a bond with the steel, and the stearate soap forms a bond with the phosphate, is very effective, and additional lubricants such as graphite or molybdenum disulphide are only used for particularly difficult forgings.

ADVANTAGES OF PROCESS

That the cold-forging industry has grown to its present size indicates that its products have supplied a growing need of industry for components that are either completely finished, forged to size, or have a guaranteed minimum amount of material for machining, with close tolerances for automatic machine loading and locations.

Cold forgings produced from hot-worked wrought bar subjected to the further cold work inherent in the process have a dense, continuous structure with no hard scale or skin, permitting high machining speeds, with even cutting pressures giving good tool life. As no forging draft angles are required, the components are closer to the finished shape, and correspondingly lighter than the equivalent hot-forged part. The initial slug weight is frequently the same as the finished forging, as little material is lost in annealing scale and no forging flash is needed.

An example of a bevel pinion produced by cold forging, together with the finished machined component is shown in Fig. 2, and a range of components currently produced by the cold-forging process is shown in Fig. 3.

TOLERANCES

Tolerance bands on the diameters of cold forged parts can be held to 0·4% of the diameter (0·1 mm on 25 mm). A tolerance band of 0·5% (0·125 mm on 25 mm) on lengths, is possible for dimensions contained within the punch or die assemblies.

Larger tolerances of about 0·50 mm are required across the tool parting line between punch and die. The concentricity of features within the punch or die is a function of the accuracy of the toolmaking. Concentricity betwen punch and die is dependent upon the accuracy of the press frame, ram guidance system, and the type of press-die set employed; tolerances of 0·10 mm diameter are possible, but a tolerance of 0·30 mm is more practical.

Straightness is dependent upon the type of forging method used, but can be as close as 0·1% of the length (0·025 mm on 25 mm) for some tubular sections. The surface

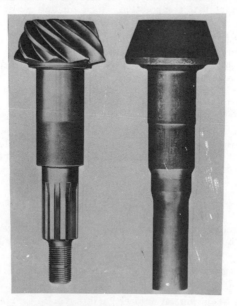

2 Cold-forged bevel pinion

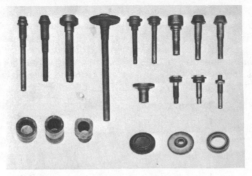

3 Selection of cold-forged parts

finish of the forgings is good as long as the zinc phosphate coat is not removed, with finishes of 32 CLA or lower being attainable.

APPLICATIONS AND MATERIALS

Low- and medium-carbon steels are generally used for cold-forged parts; high-carbon and low-alloy steels are also used, but as forging pressures are higher and tool loading greater, the type of part formed is more restricted.

The microstructure and surface quality of the steel slug is usually more significant to successful cold forging than composition. Good surface quality in the steel bar is essential, and no laps or seams can be permitted as these will cause the forging to tear under the forging pressure.

The best steel for cold forming is one that is soft, has well dispersed carbides, and a homogeneous grain structure not exceeding McQuaid-Ehn grain size no. 5 (256 grains/mm^2). The effects of residual and alloy elements must also be considered, such as the hardening effects of carbon and manganese, and these constituents must be kept as low as possible. A clean material is required, and vacuum-degassed steels have been found to give good results for cold forging.

The steels suitable for cold forging can be placed into three groups, as shown in Table 1. From this range of steels it is possible to select a material with characteristics to cover most design applications; it is also possible to forge some types of stainless steel, En58 or ASIA305, into simple designs.

MANUFACTURING METHOD

The majority of steel cold forged parts over 0·5 kg in weight are produced from round, hot-rolled black bar specified cold forging quality, normally supplied in lengths of 12—14 ft.

A typical manufacturing sequence for a cold-forged gas bottle is shown in Fig. 4; the individual operations are as follows.

The first operation is to cut the bar into slugs; this can be carried out on either a circular cold saw or band sawing machine. These processes have the disadvantages

Table 1 Suitability of steels for cold forming

En grades	Characteristics	Applications
Group A 2E 32A 201	Easy to forge; will give as-forged yield strengths of 6 ton/cm^2; slugs do not require annealing	Drive shaft flanges, valve spring retainers, brake pistons, brake adjusters, water pump hubs, hydraulic ram bases, spur gears
Group B 8B 16 18C (also BS3111)	More difficult to forge; used mainly for solid parts, subsequently through hardened; slugs may require annealing	Half-shafts, ball joint studs, motor and generator shafts, tie rods, push rods, wheel bolts, stub axles
Group C 206 361, 362 351, 352 325, 34	Easier to forge than the higher carbon steels, parts subsequently case hardened; slugs may require annealing	Main drive gears, gearbox main shafts, piston pins, needle bearing cups, bevel gears, bevel pinions, helical gears

4 Manufacturing sequence for gas bottle, low-carbon steel

of wasting material in the form of cutting swarf, and are slow in operation. Sawing is, however, reliable and is widely used for cheaper low-carbon steel slugs, particularly where the length of the slug is smaller than the diameter. For medium-carbon or alloy steel slugs cold cropping is employed on either a billet shearing machine or more generally a shearing unit used in a vertical mechanical press.

The slugs are prepared for forging by subcritical or spheroidal annealing, dependent upon the steel analysis and original bar condition, followed by mechanical removal of the annealing or bar scale, and cutting burrs by tumbling, vibrating, or shot blasting. The slugs are then ready for the application of the zinc phosphate/stearate soap lubricant. The component is produced on a hydraulic press designed for the process, which can be manually or automatically fed.

Two or more forging operations can often be carried out without need for interstage annealing to relieve work hardening or the application of additional lubricant. In this case interstage subcritical annealing and phosphating is required between the reverse-extruding and forward-extruding operations, but not between the forward-extruding and final forging operation for closing the neck. The bottle is completed by machining the flange and thread cutting.

As the working pressure on the cold-forging tools can be high, and considerable friction generated between slug and tools, wear on tooling working faces can be a critical factor in economic production runs. The tools are, therefore, constructed of easily replaceable punches and dies, in Swedish tool steels or carbides fitted into interchangeable die support rings and press die sets. A typical tooling layout for producing the gas bottle is shown in Fig. 5; with such systems tool changeover times can be controlled and tooling replacement costs kept low.

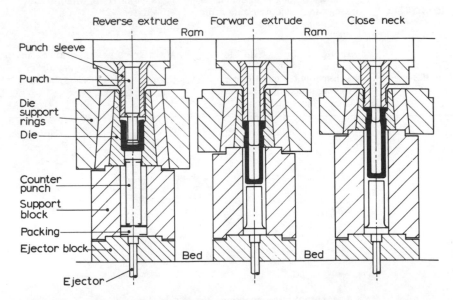

5 Three-operation tooling layout for gas bottle

A component ideal for cold forging in two stations without interstage treatments, is the automotive manual gearbox main drive gear (first motion shaft). The manufacturing sequence is shown in Fig. 6 and the tooling layout in Fig. 7. The individual operations are as follows:

The slug is cropped from the bar in a shearing unit. It is important that the slug shear face is square to the slug axis, and is clean with no tears, as any defects can cause trouble in later machining or heat-treatment operations. Because of the alloy content of the material it is necessary to anneal the slug, and a spheroidize annealing operation is carried out in an atmosphere controlled furnace.

The slug is descaled, phosphated for lubrication, and forged in two operations on either hydraulic or mechanical presses, the first station being to double-reduce the shank by forward extrusion, the second station completing the component. This

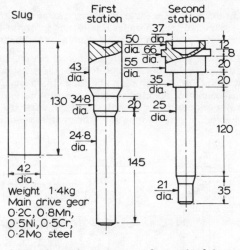

6 **Manufacturing sequence for main drive gear**

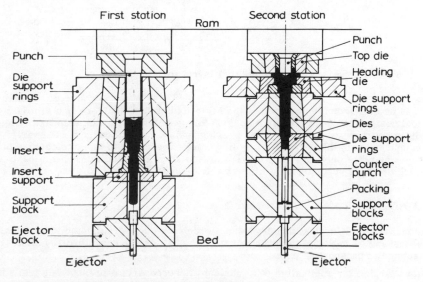

7 **Two-station tooling layout for main drive gear**

second operation is an example of a forging incorporating all three types of basic extrusion: a reverse-extruded top, an upset flange, and a forward-extruded shank. The component is completed by machining, hardening, and grinding operations.

An example of a hollow part produced by simultaneous reverse and forward extrusion of the same section is the automotive piston pin; the manufacturing sequence and tool layout is shown in Fig. 8. The pins are forged in a single operation from sawn, annealed, descaled, and phosphated slugs on an automatically fed mechanical press. The centre web is removed by piercing, and the ends are machined to the required form, and the component is completed by case hardening and grinding on the outside diameter.

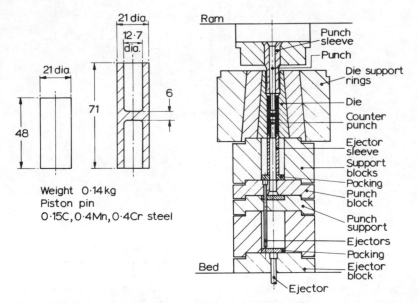

8 **Manufacturing sequence and tool layout for piston pin**

As can be seen from comparison of the three tooling layouts, there is a similarity in tool design and construction. It is therefore practical to design standard ranges of die support rings, support blocks, packing, and ejectors to cover a wide variety of components. In this way initial tooling can be restricted to the manufacture of punches and dies only, and the cost kept to a minimum. In addition, when a particular forging becomes obsolete, most of the tooling can be re-used.

PLANT

The modern cold-forging industry uses a wide range of hydraulic and mechanical presses; and examples of the six most important types are described, together with an automatic phosphating plant.

Before forging, the application of a lubricant is necessary; at present this takes the form of zinc phosphate, and a typical plant is shown in Fig. 9. This is an automatic

9 Automatic phosphating plant

process plant which involves the immersion of the steel slug or forging for controlled periods in an alkali cleaner, or if necessary an acid pickle, followed by cold and hot water rinses, phosphating solution further rinses, and a stearate soap solution.

The most widely used forging press is the vertical single-station mechanical crank press with capacities ranging from 250—1 500 tonf. These presses are specifically designed for the process, and are generally of tie rod construction; they incorporate deep rams for adequate guidance usually with overload devices in the form of shear plates. The presses have mechanical ejector systems linked to the ram movement, and they are driven by electric motor through flywheels, helical reduction gears, and multi-disk clutches and brakes. The ram strokes range from 250—1 000 mm, with ejector movements of about half the ram stroke; a typical press is shown in Fig. 10. These presses can produce a wide range of forgings from 0·25—10 kg in weight; up to 500 mm in length; with diameters of 125 mm in low-carbon steel. They can be both manually and automatically fed, and production rates vary from 200—1 200/h.

The second most widely used press is the vertical single-station hydraulic, with capacities ranging 500—5 000 tonf. These presses have generally the same specification as their mechanical counterparts, apart from their power system. Hydraulic presses can produce larger forgings than mechanical presses, but are slower in operation, with production rates of up to 300/h. They are used for manufacturing forgings of up to 20 kg in weight and 200 mm in diameter in low-carbon steel, and are considered less damaging to tooling since no impact loads are applied, and maximum working pressures can be closely controlled. An example of a hydraulic

10 750 tonf W and M mechanical press   11 5 000 tonf ASEA hydraulic press

press is shown in Fig. 11; this particular type is unique in that a wire-wound press
frame is utilized in place of a tie rod or welded fabrication.

A new type of mechanical press just being introduced is the vertical twin-station
mechanical press as manufactured by B. and S. Massey Ltd, shown in Fig. 12. This
press of 750 tonf capacity and 400 mm ram stroke, has two stations, as shown in
Fig. 13, with automatic loading of each station, and is particularly suited to the
manufacture of high-quantity shafts and bevel pinions where no interstage heat
treatment or lubrication is required.

Another type of multi-station press is the four-station 250 ton capacity horizontal
hydraulic extrusion press, as shown in Fig. 14. Designed for the production of
flanged shafts of up to 55 mm shank diameter and 1m in length, this particular unit
uses an automatic transfer mechanism between the working stations, which progressively reduces the diameter and increases the length of the shank. A hot-upset
forging is used as the raw material for this application but a cold-forged blank
could also be utilized.

Large quantity, complex forgings can be produced on horizontal three-, four- or
five-station cold-forging machines. These presses of up to 1 400 tonf capacity using
either bright-drawn, annealed, and phosphated wire in coils or pre-cut slugs as raw
material, are very efficient since the component is produced entirely on the press
with no interstage treatment or handling. A typical unit is shown in Fig. 15, and
forgings can be produced at rates of from 1 500—6 000/h.

An alternative type of multiple-blow cold-forging press suitable for smaller forgings
up to 0·15 kg in weight, 37 mm in diameter, 100 mm in length, is the two-station,

12 750 tonf Massey Schlatter twin-
station mechanical press

13 Twin-tool stations showing bevel
pinion forging operations

three-forging blow machine, shown in Fig. 16. In this type of press the workpiece
is automatically transferred between the two forging dies, at the second die station
the component can be struck twice with different punches, thus increasing the
capacity of the machine to produce larger or more complex forgings. These
machines, using bright-drawn, annealed, and phosphate steel wire as feed stock,
with slug cutting-off carried out automatically on the press, can produce over 6 000
forgings every hour.

14 250 tonf USl clearing four-station
hydraulic press

15 1375 tonf four-station mechanical
cold-forging machine

ECONOMICS

The most economic parts for cold forging are those that can be produced on the
multiple-blow cold-forging machines, leaving little or no subsequent operations.
Wheel bolts, studs, and sparking plug bodies are good examples of this type of part,
as only thread rolling, heat treatment, and plating are necessary to finish the
components.

16 Ray Carl two-station, three-blow mechanical press

As the capital cost of such plant is high, and the setting time relatively long, minimum production runs of over 50 000 parts are generally required to justify the use of this type of equipment.

Another range of parts which can show considerable savings are shafts where the length—diameter ratio is large; and flanges where head sizes can be much greater than shank diameters. These components can be produced economically on single-station plant with minimum quantities as low as 1 000 parts.

As with hot forging, the raw material cost forms the largest proportion of the forging cost. A balance must therefore be struck between the number of forging operations, to remove the maximum amount of material and thus giving the closest possible shape to the finished design, and the cost of the forging and interstage operations.

It is often not economic to do more than two forging press operations, particularly if interstage treatments are necessary, but with the continuing increase in the cost of steel the multiple-operation cold forging becomes more feasible.

CONCLUSIONS

The cold-forging industry is basically a product of technological change and the need to reduce manufacturing costs; it is gaining importance as raw material and labour costs continue to rise. Components that were not economic for the process a few years ago are now being cold forged.

In order that the industry's products can be used to maximum advantage it is important that all connected with the manufacturing industries should have some knowledge of the cold-forging technique.

It is particularly important for a close relationship to be developed between the Component Design Engineer and the Cold-Forging Engineer. Only in this way can the full advantages of cold-forged components be exploited, and the optimum design achieved at the lowest possible cost.

ACKNOWLEDGMENTS

Acknowledgment is made to the following companies for kindly providing photographs:
ASEA (GB) Ltd; J. Brockhouse and Co. Ltd; Rockwell Machine Tool Co. Ltd; Wilkins
and Mitchell Ltd; B. and S. Massey Ltd; GKN Screws and Fasteners Ltd.

SOME NEWER HOT FORMING PROCESSES

W. Johnson and J. B. Hawkyard

This paper briefly reviews a few selected developments in materials, machines, and forming techniques, some of which are still in the laboratory, and others at various stages of evaluation by industry.

It is often difficult to foresee the eventual extent to which industry can accept and absorb a new and promising development, particularly when it is in competition with established methods which are themselves being steadily impoved. Where the new development is competing in this way the outcome is determined strictly by economic considerations, calling for detailed information on machine and tool life, and reliability, usually over an extensive trial period. Very occasionally, of course, a new and revolutionary process results in a new product, for which there is a ready market, and the situation is then quite different.

Some of the recent developments to be considered as somewhat speculative insofar as their industrial potentialities are still not fully explored. It is desirable, of course, that such developments become widely known, so that 'cross-fertilization' of ideas can help in determining their proper role. New developments which may offer considerable advantage in one direction often introduce new difficulties, and it may happen, for example, that a new machine development will be found to be particularly suited to exploit newly explored material properties, thus presenting entirely new prospects.

The topics to be discussed have been chosen, as far as possible, to comply with the purpose of this particular meeting and they are also naturally determined to some extent by the research interests of the authors. It was considered at one stage that they might fall under the headings of 'machines' and 'materials', but this classification seems to be too restrictive; consequently they are considered individually, but of course not in isolation from the general picture.

HIGH-RATE FORMING

High-rate forming machines typified by Dynapak[1] and Petroforge[2] have received a great deal of development in recent years and extensive analyses have been made of their characteristics in relation to more conventional machines.

A brief survey is presented of some recent developments in forging machines, forming techniques, and special material properties of interest and possible significance to the forging industry. Various forms of rotary forging machine are outlined: for the automated production of stepped shafts, for example, and for performing upset forging at reduced loads by imparting a rocking motion to one of the die members. The new material properties include superplasticity, a condition which provides greatly increased formability, and thermomechanical treatments which give increased strengths to steels as a result of combining heat treatment with mechanical working. Other new forming processes include bubble casting for producing thin-walled containers direct from the molten state, and extrusion moulding for making intricate shapes.

Both authors are in the Mechanical Engineering Department of University of Manchester Institute of Science and Technology
621.974.8.016.2

Apart from the claimed compactness and lower cost of the machines for a given energy output, they have been shown to offer certain advantages in hot forging, well documented now,[3,4,5,6] relating mainly to reduced workpiece cooling and improved lubrication, thus offering the possibility of forming thinner and more intricate shapes in fewer operations, and with minimum subsequent machining.

The attendant disadvantages and difficulties of the high-rate machines are also fairly well known, though perhaps less well publicized, and the extent to which they eventually become established remains to be seen. At present they appear to be used for rather specialized applications, and mainly in research and development fields. It has been suggested[7] that the ability of the high-rate machines to form a component in a single stroke, combined with the accurate control of energy output, should make them suited to automated production, and future development would be expected to occur in this direction.

Largely through the advent of these machines, considerable research work has been directed into various aspects of press forging, which is generally beneficial, leading to increased knowledge also of conventional processes.

The yield behaviour of metals at high temperature and strain rate has received further attention, particularly in relation to the effects of friction and heat flow between the hot work material and die surfaces.[5,8] It is established that metals are generally very sensitive to strain rate at high temperature, so that they show considerable increase in flow resistance when deformed at high strain rate. Energy requirements increase with forming speed on this account, but there is some compensation due to reduced heat losses to the tools, and reduced friction.

A problem that arises with high-velocity impact machines is the damage that can occur to the machine structure and tooling due to the shock loading. This appears to be due, at least in part, to stress-wave effects in various machine members. Stress-wave magnitudes are dependent on impact velocity, and there has been a tendency for later machines to operate at rather lower maximum velocities than earlier models.

The evaluation of tool life in the high-rate hot-forging machines is a highly complex matter, depending on the interrelation of lubrication, scale formation, flow stress, forging time, and total contact time between the workpiece and dies, and it appears that no simple general conclusion can be drawn regarding the effects of speed. The various factors are discussed in detail in a recently published book on high-speed metal forming.[7]

ROTARY FORGING MACHINES

Developments are taking place in special forging machines in which the predominant motion is other than an axial squeeze, and brief mention will be made of some processes which, although having quite different modes of operation, can each be regarded as rotary forging.

The first represents a development of the forging press, aimed at reducing the size and capital cost by lessening the load necessary to form a given product. The principle is shown schematically in Fig. 1, for a simple upsetting operation. Instead of the direct squeeze of a conventional press, the workpiece is subjected to a combined rolling and squeezing action between a flat bottom platen and a swivelling upper die, with a conical working face. The cone axis is inclined so that the narrow sector in contact with the workpiece is parallel to the lower platen, and as the cone axis rotates about the cone apex, the contact zone also rotates. At the same time, the lower platen

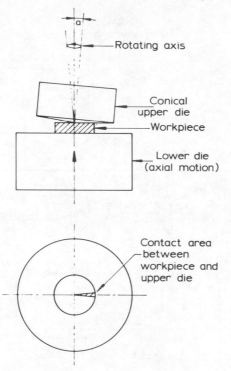

1 Principle of rotary forging press

is moved forward axially so that the workpiece is progressively compressed by the rolling action. Press loading is appreciably less than with a direct squeeze because of the relatively small area of instantaneous contact. The method should be particularly suited to the forging of circular components with thin intricate flange sections. The process was patented by H. F. Massey[9] in 1929, but it appears to have remained unexploited since that time until quite recently. A paper has recently been published by the Institution of Mechanical Engineers describing development in this country.[10] Experimental equipment for this work is shown in Fig. 2. Similar investigations are in progress also in Poland.

Another quite different type of rotary forging machine[11] is a development of the swaging machine, using the impact of a set of three or four radially opposed hammers to reduce the diameter of bar or tube in any desired manner as it is fed between them. This allows the manufacture of stepped and tapered shafts to be performed with very simple dies. The machines are particularly suitable for short production runs of components that otherwise would be extruded or upset-forged, the principal advantage being that tooling is less expensive.

A type of rotary forging machine known as the wedge roll hot-forming machine[12] performs the same sort of task as the swaging machine mentioned above, in producing stepped and tapered sections, but by a radically different process. The wedge roll action can be likened somewhat to a thread rolling machine, where round bar

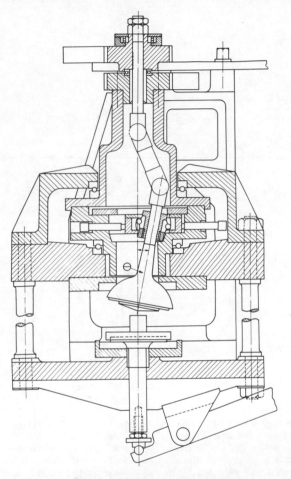

**2 Experimental rotary forging press. Parts
can be identified by referring to reference 10**

is rolled in the gap between two parallel rolls rotating in the same direction, so that
the workpiece is impressed with the roll form. The wedge roll machine performs
its forming action within a fraction of one revolution of the rolls by tooling which is
bolted onto the rolls (see Fig. 3). Typical components produced by the process are
shown in Fig. 4.

The machine is suitable for automatic production, using bar stock automatically fed
to the rolls through an induction heating unit. Material utilization is 100%, and forming accuracy is said to be in the region of 0·004 in.

Another form of this rolling process, again resembling thread rolling to some extent,
is used to produce steel balls and rollers direct from bar stock (Fig. 5). The heated
bar is continuously fed between two rolls, with fixed centres, the shape being progressively developed until it becomes 'parted off' at the exit.[13]

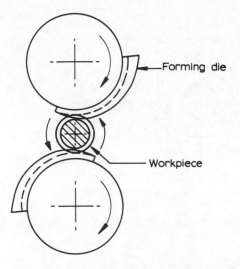

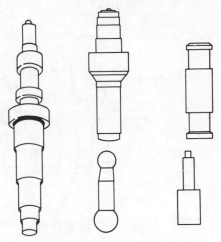

3 Principle of wedge roll hot forming

4 Typical products of wedge roll hot forming

Stepped shafts are also manufactured by the rolling processes illustrated in Fig. 6.[13] The heated blank is rotated by a chuck and fed axially between three forming rolls, spaced at 120°, the radial positions being controlled by a template to produce the required profile. The process is somewhat similar to copyturning, with the important difference that material is displaced rather than removed, and material utilization approaches 100% overall. Accuracy is said to be within 0·015in per inch of diameter and shoulder positions can be held to within 0·06in. The fatigue strength of the products is said to be better than for turned or conventionally forged parts[13].

RING ROLLING

Although ring rolling is by no means a new forming process insofar as it has been employed for many years in the manufacture of steel tyres for railway rolling stock and similar types of product, in recent years mills have been developed to produce more complex axisymmetric shapes[14] and they are now used to form products such as weld neck pipe flanges and gas turbine rings in a variety of alloys.

The rolling process usually involves appreciable increase in diameter of the workpiece, starting perhaps from a pierced billet. Another recent development would perhaps be more accurately termed form rolling, involving little or no increase in diameter as the required profile is accurately impressed on a tubular workpiece.

EXTRUSION MOULDING

A new process, which may find limited application in the rather specialized field of precision forming of difficult metals, is known as extrusion moulding, or kinetic moulding. It employs the principle, in common with most explosive forming opera-

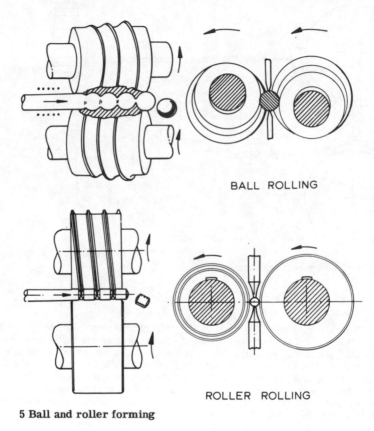

BALL   ROLLING

ROLLER   ROLLING

5 Ball and roller forming

tions, of initially imparting a high velocity to the workpiece, the kinetic energy then being progressively transformed into plastic work. In extrusion moulding the high velocity is achieved by forward extrusion under a high-speed hammer, the extruded product being projected into a mould, which it normally fills with a high degree of efficiency. The extremities of the mould, normally the most difficult to fill in a conventional process, tend to become filled first as the metal impinges on the die faces. The extrusion billet is initially heated, and the plastic work expended during the extrusion stage produces further heating.

The process was first outlined by the General Dynamics Corporation of America[15] and studies have been made in this country at the NEL[16,17], and at the University of Strathclyde[18] on the somewhat similar process utilizing a gun for accelerating the billet.

The main attraction in this process would appear to be the excellent die filling for intricate shapes, with good reproduction of fine texture on the die surface.

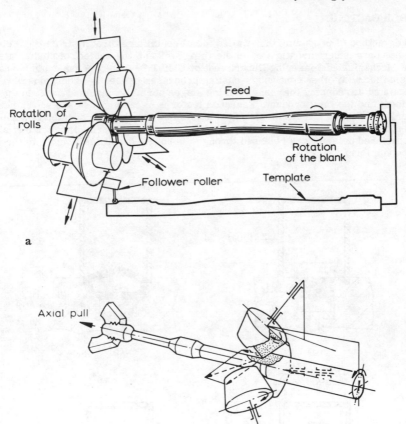

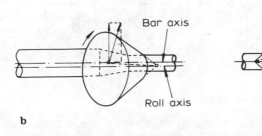

a *parallel axis rolls*; b *inclined axis rolls*

6 Transverse rolling of shafts

BUBBLE CASTING

A novel method of producing thin-walled metal containers directly from the molten state has been under investigation in the USA,[19],[20] and the subject of studies also in the Mechanical Engineering Department of UMIST.[21] The process could perhaps be classified with other continuous-casting processes presently undergoing development, aimed at reducing the many forming stages normally involved between the cast ingot and the final product. Essential features of the process are shown schematically in Fig. 7. A multi-orifice nozzle is situated below the surface of a bath of molten metal, with a forming mould positioned, mouth downwards, immediately above it. A metered pulse of gas released through the nozzle displaces liquid into the mould in a bubble form.

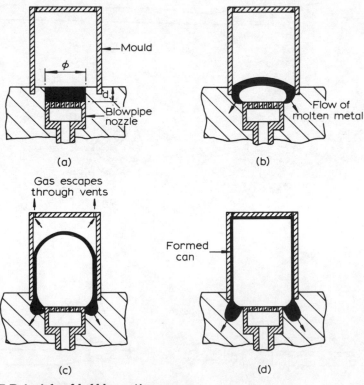

7 Principle of bubble casting process

A proportion of the liquid flows back to the melt and the remainder freezes on contact with the cool mould wall, yielding a thin-walled vessel with the shape of the mould. The rapid quench produces a fine, strong grain structure. The process has not as yet been applied commercially to compete with conventional methods, in terms of uniformity of walls and soundness, but the potential is evident, particularly for the production of asymmetrical re-entrant shapes which are difficult to form by more conventional methods. The versatility in this respect should be similar to glass blowing.

The process is being applied at present to aluminium and its alloys, and an essential feature is the composition of the forming gas, which contains a small proportion of oxygen for creating oxide films to support the expanding bubble. Without the oxygen the gas issues from the nozzle as a large number of separate bubbles and the forming does not occur. It is not known whether the process might be applied to other metals.

WARM FORGING

Forming metals at temperatures below the normal hot-working range offers certain potential advantages over either hot or cold forming, in that there can be significant reductions in forming loads as compared with cold working, while the problems of scaling and decarburization of steels, encountered with hot forming, can be avoided. More effective lubrication can be achieved than with hot forming; draft angles can be reduced, and extrusion carried out as well as upsetting. Forgings can be produced to greater accuracy, with reduced machining allowances.

The yield strength of the workpiece will be higher than in the hot-forging condition, so that die materials will generally need to be stronger and the process is likely to resemble cold-forming practice rather than hot.[22] For some materials there may be limitations due to reduced ductility at certain temperatures.

Warm forging appears to have found little application commercially, and the economics are difficult to assess, mainly due to lack of information on tool life. It is possible that it may eventually be linked most suitably with one of the newer forming machines, such as the rotary forging press, which gives reduced forging loads.

THERMOMECHANICAL TREATMENTS

The combination of mechanical working with heat treatment, to improve strength properties of steels, appears to have been first reported only 15 years ago,[23] and developments have taken place mainly within the last 10 years.

The treatments can be broadly classified into two categories, first the mechanical working of austenite below the normal hot-working temperature range, so that recrystallization does not occur during forming, followed immediately by quenching and tempering (ausforming), and second deformation after quenching, usually at elevated temperature in combination with tempering.

The increases in strength reported[24,25,26] for various alloy steels have been substantial, typically in the 10—30% range, depending on forming temperature and amount of deformation, and other characteristics such as fatigue life and toughness are also generally improved.

The ausforming process has been applied successfully to various metalworking methods such as rolling, forging, and extrusion.[24] The operating conditions are somewhat more exacting and critical than for conventional procedures, of course. There are narrower limits on forming temperature and time, to avoid pearlite formation; forming pressures are greater than at normal temperatures, and since the part is quenched immediately after forming, the range of machining and finishing operations is limited.

Practical applications at present seem to be mainly in the aircraft and armament industries, in the production of high-strength forgings and armour.

There is an evident overlap between ausforging and warm forging, described above, and the advantages of improved lubrication and reduced scaling might be achieved, providing the billet can be adequately protected from oxidation during the initial high-temperature austenitizing treatment.

The second process, involving the mechanical working of martensite during tempering, appears to be applicable mainly to the manufacture of high-tensile drawn products, such as reinforcing rods.

Figure 8 shows the gain in strength reported[26] for steel, SAE4140 (0·4C—0·9Mn—1·0Cr—0·2Mo) deformed 14% in martensitic condition at various drawing temperatures. The gain shown is the difference between the strength after drawing, and after tempering at that same temperature without drawing. At 300 °C the increase in yield stress is quite substantial, at about 25 tonf/in².

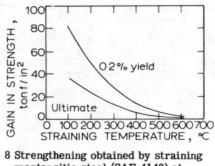

8 Strengthening obtained by straining martensitic steel (SAE 4140) at elevated temperatures

SUPERPLASTIC METAL FORMING

Superplastic forming can be regarded as another warm-working process in that it takes place at an absolute temperature of about half the melting point, but in this case the material is in a special metallurgical state and it displays special properties.

Investigations into the fundamental properties and commercial prospects of superplastic alloys have been very active in recent years, and although this field of metal forming appears to be still largely exploratory, it will undoubtedly assume increased importance.

Superplastic alloys have the capacity of undergoing very large extensions, as compared with normal metals, in operations such as stretch forming and blow moulding, as well as in simple tension, where extensions of several hundred percent may be achieved. The superplastic property may be produced by thermal cycling about a transformation temperature during the straining process (termed transformation superplasticity) or by developing a very fine stable microstructure by suitable heat treatment or mechanical working (micrograin superplasticity) and deforming at a temperature of about half the absolute melting temperature.

Micrograin superplasticity is the most industrially significant, and present development work is mainly in this field. The grain diameter is very small, in the region of 1—2 μm as compared with 10—1 000 μm for normal metals, the structure is equiaxed, and in this condition the superplastic material shows negligible strain hardening yet a very marked sensitivity to strain rate. In this respect it can be likened to molten glass, which shows comparable forming behaviour.

A yield stress-strain rate relationship for a metal in the superplastic condition is shown in Fig. 9 for comparison with the normal as-cast state.[27]

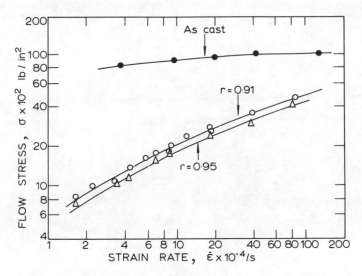

9 Yield stress-strain rate relationships for a tin-lead alloy in the superplastic and as-cast condition; superplastic material extruded at reduction r

A six fold increase in yield stress can be observed over the strain rate range, and at the lower end of the range the yield stress is only one tenth that of the as-cast material. This latter observation illustrates the pronounced capcity of the super-plastic to be 'creep formed' at relatively low loads.

Materials

A large number of superplastic alloys are known, eutectic and euctectoid alloys being among the first studied. Some eutectic alloys of tin are superplastic at room temperature, making them useful for experimental studies. Euctectoid zinc-aluminium alloys, basically 78Zn-22Al, which are superplastic at about 250°C, are receiving considerable attention in the automobile field for the manufacture of body panels, under the name of Prestal.[28]

In addition to eutectic and euctectoid alloys, other materials have been obtained in the superplastic state such as nickel and chrome steels, titanium and zirconium alloys, aluminium alloys, nickel, copper, and zinc alloys.

Attempts to make mild steel, brass, and common aluminium alloys superplastic have so far been only partially successful.

Forming applications

Forming rates are low compared with normal processes; forming times would typically be in the region of several minutes, and pressures would be significantly lower than normal, by a factor of perhaps 10.

Sheet forming techniques which have been applied to superplastic materials include vacuum forming, stretch forming, and blow moulding, as used for glass and plastic products. The high degree of formability which can be achieved is illustrated in Fig. 10.

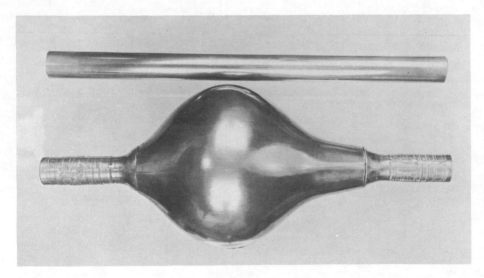

10 Tube of superplastic tin-lead alloy expanded by internal pressure

In addition to the work on sheet-metal forming, some exploratory work has been carried out into creep forming in compression,[29] which illustrates clearly the exceptional strain rate sensitivity, and indicates further possible applications. The results of coining tests, using zinc-aluminium as the die material, are shown in Fig. 11. A threepenny piece was used as a pattern (Fig. 11*a*) to coin a die in superplastic zinc-aluminium (Fig. 11*b*) at a temperature of 265°C and under a load of 130 lbf applied for 5 min. After cooling to room temperature the die was then used in a drop hammer to strike impressions in copper (Fig. 11*c*). The experiment demonstrated that intricate detail could be produced by very modest loads, about 300 lbf/in^2 mean pressure, but at room temperature and under dynamic loading the strength was evidently very high.

Apart from the investigations into the lead-tin and aluminium-zinc alloys some research work has been reported on a titanium alloy at 925°C, and on stainless steel at 940°C,[30] involving the hydrostatic bulging of clamped sheet into shaped moulds.

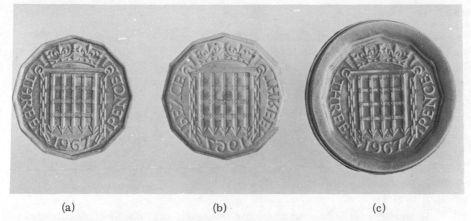

(a)   (b)   (c)

a original pattern (threepenny bit); b *die formed in superplastic Zn-Al at 265°C by impressing with a under 130 lbf steady load;* c *impression formed in copper using superplastic die (b) under drop hammer*

11 Coining experiment using a superplastic Zn-Al die

Practical applications of these and other alloys which are superplastic at high temperatures appear to be very limited at present. A recent review of the present situation and future possibilities is given by Nicholson.[31]

Commercial uses

The future role of superplastic alloys in industry is at present seen as being mainly in the manufacture of complex sheet-metal forms using relatively simple and inexpensive tooling and equipment. In the car industry it may find a role in the lower volume production range, for sports car bodywork for example, where conventional tooling costs are relatively high because of the small scale of production. Superplastics display the same sort of formability as thermoplastics in certain sheet-forming processes, and it is likely that they will replace plastics to some extent, offering advantages in strength and elastic modulus, and also cost, when production is on a commercial scale.

In considering the use of a superplastic alloy it must be remembered that its special metallurgical condition may make it susceptible to creep in service. A metal which has a high superplastic forming temperature, such as the stainless steel and titanium alloy mentioned above, has satisfactory room-temperature strength because of the large temperature differential, but in the other extreme the lead—tin eutectoid, super plastic at room temperature, would obviously show very marked creep behaviour in room-temperature service. Likewise the range of alloys based on aluminium, zinc, and magnesium, formed in the 200—450°C range, would also be susceptible to creep at room temperature. To overcome this problem the material can either be given a final heat treatment, to convert the structure to the normal condition, and this would generally entail further manufacturing cost, or the alloy composition might be 'tailored' to give improved service properties, possibly at the expense of slightly reduced superplastic behaviour. These problems are being actively investigated at present.[31,32]

REFERENCES

1   W. G. Mang: *Sheet Metal Ind,* 1962, **39**, 424, 541
2   L. T. Chan *et al.*: *Proc. IME,* 1965, **180**, Pt. 1
3   S. A. Skeen: *Machinery* (London) 1965, **107**, 228
4   E. A. Welky and C. T. Syburg: *Machinery* (New York) 1965, **71**, 101
5   S. C. Jain and A. N. Bramley: *Proc. IME.,* 1968, **182**, 783
6   S. C. Jain and A. N. Bramley: Proc. 9th Mach. Tool Des. Res. Conf., Birmingham, 1968, 95
7   R. Davies and E. R. Austin: 'Developments in high-speed metal forming', 1970, London, The Machinery Publishing Co. Ltd.
8   M. A. Kellow *et al.*: Proc 9th Mach. Tool Des. Res. Conf., Birmingham, 1968
9   H. F. Massey: Brit. Pat. 319065, 1929
10 R. A. C. Slater *et al.*: *Proc. IME,* 1970
11 A. M. Sabroff *et al.*: 'Forging materials and practices; 1968, New York, Reinhold Book Corporation
12 Anon: *Engineering,* 1969, **207**, 5364, 280
13 Anon: *The Engineer,* 1967, **224**, 5833, 611
14 Anon: *Engineering,* 1969, **207**, 5364, 284
15 E. W. Fedderson: *SAEJ,* 1960, **68**, 5, 39
16 R. J. Dower: NEL Rep. 214, 1966
17 R. J. Dower: NEL Rep. 455, 1970
18 F. W. Travis: *Int. J. Mach. Tool Des. Res.,* 1969, **9**, 51
19 Anon: *Iron Age,* 1963, **191**, 69
20 Brit. Pat. 1048473
21 D. Horrocks *et al.*: *Proc. IME.,* 1970
22 J. A. Luntz: 'The exploitation of new materials and new processes in the forging industry,' Inst. of Metallurgists Review Course, Series 2, 3, 1969
23 E. M. H. Lips and H. van Zuilen: *Metal Progress,* 1954, **66**, 2, 103
24 W. M. Justasson and R. Clark: Metallurgical Society Conference, AIME, 1965, Pittsburgh, **44**, 481
25 C. W. Marshall, *et al*: Metallurgical Society Conference, AIME, 1965, Pittsburgh, **44**, 515
26 J. L. Peterson and E. S. Nachtman: Metallurgical Society Conference, AIME, 1965, Pittsburgh, **44**, 549
27 T. Y. M. Al-Naib and J. L. Duncan: *Int. J. Mech. Sci.,* 1970, **12**, 463
28 D. North: Inst. of Sheet Metal Engineering Colloquium, Birmingham, March, 1969
29 R. A. Saller and J. L. Duncan: *JIM,* to be published
30 G. C. Cornfield and R. H. Johnson: *Int. J. Mech. Sci.,* 1970, **12**, 479
31 R. B. Nicholson: Inst. of Metallurgists Review Course, Series 2, 3, 1969
32 H. Naziri and R. Pearce: *Int. J. Mech. Sci.,* 1970, **12**, 513

DISCUSSION OF THE FIRST SESSION

In the chair: **Mr R. Rajan** (British Leyland)

Mr W. J. Cumberland (Automotive Products Limited): How near are we to having a production machine for the rotary forging press?

Dr Hawkyard: You will have to approach Massey's for that information; I can only say that they have had a prototype running for some time.

The Chairman: I believe that Massey's have had a press like this for some time, and I am pretty certain that if you want to talk about it seriously they would be happy to do so.

Mr W. Beattie (Lamberton and Co. Ltd): My question is directed to Mr Thornton, although it applies equally to most of the papers being presented today. With hot forging, the raw material cost forms a high proportion of the forging cost. I am rather surprised to find that in none of the papers presented today has there been any mention of how some savings could be achieved in raw materials. Bar and ingot stock from steel mills varies considerably in cross-section, and the time-honoured method of cutting slugs is to crop to length. This method can be uneconomical due to the varying cross-sections. Computerized schemes are available today where bars are monitored when they come to the shearing machine, and measuring stops are set not to cut a length, of material, but a correct volume. Would you care to comment?

Mr. Thornton: I do not really understand the basic premise of this. As far as cold forging is concerned I have not found that the raw material does vary a great deal from mill to mill. There are certain mills in the British Steel Corporation which now specialize in cold-forging steels. I have found the quality of material from the mill at Tynsley Park to be very good. Regarding parting it off, I do not think it would make any difference whether the steel men cut it off, or whether you dealt with it in the factory itself.

Mr W. Beattie: Possibly with cold forging stock you pay a premium to get a good quality. You have suggested here that with hot forging, bar stock tends to vary as much as $2\frac{1}{2}\%$ up or down about a mean value, and this is a problem that faces people who cut to length. The more accurate the metal they crop, the less arduous the work on the dies becomes.

Professor E. C. Rollason (School of Metallurgy, University of Birmingham): We saw one slide using hydrostatic compression, but in none of the papers have we had any reference to hydrostatic extrusion. I have heard of cases where this is being done in in the warm state as well as in the cold. One interesting example was the extrusion of helical gear stock which is possible with a fluted die, and with a hydrostatic system in which the billet can rotate in the fluid. Have any of the authors any contact with this kind of process and any experience with it?

Mr Thornton: This process is being very actively investigated, and development work is in progress. There are problems with it, particularly the very high helix angle gears in manual gear boxes, which tend to give die life problems. Automatic gears could be a much better bet with this process, but it is being investigated.

The Chairman: One of the problems with extrusions that are parted off after they have been extruded is that you must be very careful with the type of component you choose. A number of the components one comes across are counter-bored at the ends, which means that if you part off you must cut your workpiece off your extrusion and then do a fantastic amount of work on the ends to bring it to the state in which you need it. In many instances the end result is not economical since the capital, labour, floor space, and so on, which you hoped you might save do not materialize.

Mr K.E.Stanley (Walterisation Company Ltd.): I should like to go a little further with your remarks on hydrostatic extrusion, Mr Chairman. As I understand it, you are correct in saying that it is really not a high-volume production proposition, and it has been chiefly confined to the forming of tools in, obviously, high-alloy steels and so on for this purpose.

I should also like to put a question on the sintered products mentioned in the powder metallurgy paper. We were given such a lot of advantages here that I began to wonder why everyone was not using the powder metallurgy form. What progress has been made with regard to the subsequent cold forging of the powder metallurgical products? In other words, coming on to the cold forging after you have actually compressed or sintered the metal?

Dr Farmer: A considerable amount of work has been done on this process. Powder metallurgists have tended in the past to take a component and then cold form it afterwards to get good tolerances and at the same time increased density. In some cases better mechanical properties are obtained. Work has been carried out on cold forming sintered slugs at NEL, by various press manufacturers, and at Birmingham University using the Petroforge machine. My own company has carried out several experiments using Dynapak equipment.

Mr D.J.Mullett (Acheson Colloids): There is little mention of the warm forging process. In my opinion the advantages of closer tolerances and reduction in scale over the hot forging process, and the lower loading and die wear over the cold forging process merits consideration of the warm forging process compared with that of hot forging. Have the authors any comments as to the future of warm forging?

Mr Thornton: Warm forging is more likely to be associated with one of the newer forming techniques, particularly Rota Forming, which I think will end up as a warm forging technique. There is no real advantage to be gained by warm forging in a press as we know it.

Dr Hawkyard: In the paper on new forming processes, the point is made that warm working will probably be associated with one of the newer processes. I showed you a slide of products made by the Massey rotary forging press; some of those were in fact produced by warm forging. I do not think that it would be practicable to warm-forge these shapes unless only a small area of the workpiece was worked on at one time, to limit tool loading.

Mr B.W.Grassam (BSC Special Steels Division): In considering gearbox components there is obviously a very big interface between two of the methods mentioned this morning: for instance, the sinter forging and cold forging, and some of the processes to be mentioned later in the day, where we are talking of 4 000 components per hour with quite close tolerances. Would the authors care to comment on which of the competitive processes they feel will win in the end, because as far as I can see they are all going for the same market?

Second, could the chairman and any of the speakers say whether they feel that the ultimate users are really encouraging capital development in the manufacturing plant, because they have got so much capital investment themselves in gear cutting machinery that they seem to have a natural reluctance to encourage some of this development?

Dr Farmer: This is a very important question. Like everything else, the newer techniques like sinter forging will find their true application in the course of time. At one stage, shell moulding, it was stated, would be the major foundry moulding process of the future. This has not proved to be the case. I think that in the gearboxes of the future one will find sintered and sinter-forged parts, as well as cold-formed and extruded parts, in addition to those produced by current methods.

Mr Thornton: It is a question of the type of part for each particular process. Cold forging and sintering do not really compete, and there are very few instances where they are strictly competitive. Mainly they are different types of parts done by cold forging and sinter forging.

Dr Farmer: The components side of the UK motor industry is also very capital-conscious. It is highly regarded in the world markets because of the quality and technological content of its products. This is shown by the fact that its direct exports, in percentage terms, are at least as high as the automobile companies themselves. One reason for this is the use of advanced processing techniques, some of which have been described today, to produce its products.

Dr D.G.Telford (Yorkshire Imperial Metals Ltd): Dr Hawkyard has mentioned in his paper the ability to 'reduce the diameter of bar and tube in any desired manner' by rotary forging. Can he consider the possible application of this process to tube manufacture?

Dr Hawkyard: The only example I can recall was using a Russian machine, and it was for producing bicycle wheel hubs from tubes in a continuous form, these being parted off subsequently. A brief description of this process is given in Ref.13 of the paper, and there is mention also of the production of bearing rings.

DEVELOPMENTS IN DROP FORGING

A. Thomas

Although the origins of closed-die forging can be traced back to Mycenae in about 1500 BC the modern drop-forging industry has developed over the last hundred years; during this time traditional plant used in the process has evolved slowly, with little radical change.

Recently however there have been rapid developments of new plant and forging techniques which are changing drop forging from a craft-based to a technologically-based industry. Some of these developments are discussed in this paper, but before their importance can be appreciated it is necessary to understand some of the principles involved in forging on conventional plant. The first part of the paper is devoted therefore to a brief study of the drop-forging process and its economics while later sections deal with new developments.

THE DROP-FORGING PROCESS

Drop forging is a metal-forming process in which hot metal is shaped in impressioned dies. It is ideally suited to the production of large numbers of identical parts such as those required by the automobile, railway, and engineering industries.

Forgings may be made from cut pieces or stamped from the end of a length of bar ('off-the-bar' forging). The forging is usually made in a number of impressions which gradually change the shape of the original bar stock to that of the finished component. This ensures that forging defects are not formed, and also aids material economy by reducing the amount of flash formed. Figure 1 shows a typical multi-impression die, and also illustrates the progressive shaping of a forging.

Drop forgings can be produced from any ductile material to almost any required shape. However, forgings with a re-entrant angles call for special techniques and are therefore costly. In addition, certain of the resulphurized and leaded steels of BS970 are not really suitable for forging. Several authors[1,2,3] have given detailed lists of ferrous and non-ferrous alloys amenable to forging.

The shape of a forging compared with that of a finished component is largely dictated by forging production requirements. To facilitate removal of the forging from the die, some draft is normally provided as shown in Fig. 2. In addition corner and fillet

The paper reviews the production of forgings on conventional plant, together with the characteristics of each plant and the economics of the forging process; different approaches to the introduction of automation and mechanical handling into the drop-forge are considered. New developments, representing a radical departure from conventional forging plant, are next considered, together with entirely new approaches to producing finished drop forgings. Finally an indication is given of the way in which the drop-forging industry may develop in the future.

The author is with the Drop Forging Research Association   621.735.043

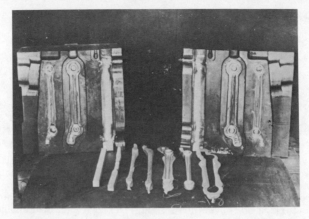

1 Typical multi-impression forging die showing the stages in production of a forging

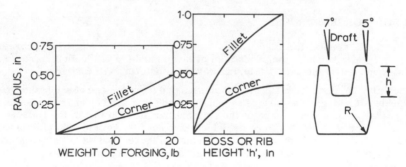

2 Draft angles and fillet radii in forging dies

radii are necessary to prevent defects and prolong die life. Typical values for such radii are indicated in Fig. 2; tolerances for drop forgings are dealt with in BS4114.

DROP-FORGING PLANT

Forgings may be made on hammers, presses, or upsetting machines, depending on the shape and size of the forging in question. The characteristics of drop-forging plant have been considered in detail by Dean,[4] but are discussed briefly below.

Hammers and friction-screw presses are characterized by a falling mass which deforms a forging until all the available energy is consumed. Machines of moderate size can produce high forging loads, and are capable of delivering large amounts of energy by the use of multiple blows. The limit of deformation of the forging is determined by chilling of the metal.[5]

The crank-press and the horizontal forging machine are constant displacement devices which build up load until the eccentric passes a bottom dead centre position. The load capacity varies throughout the crank cycle.

In hammers where the blow energy can be controlled, extensive preforming of stock by 'fullering' and 'rolling' is possible. Preforming is not generally performed on presses, and if any is required it is done on ancillary equipment such as forging rolls. The salient characteristics of various forging units are summarized in Fig. 3.

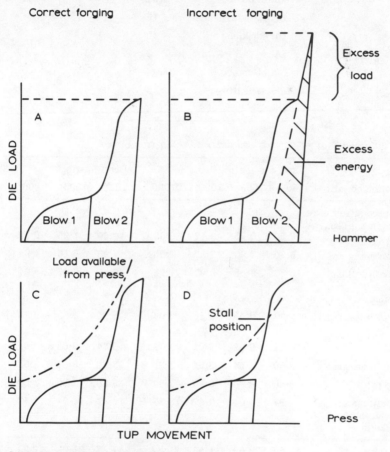

3 **Characteristics of drop-forging plant**

THE ECONOMICS OF DROP FORGING

Table 1 shows a rough breakdown of the production costs of drop-forgings. The figures are based on data collected by the Drop Forging Research Association,[6] and are useful in interpreting the effect of new developments on the economics of the forging process. Most of the developments considered affect items 1—4 in the table.

The cost structure of forgings depends of course on the number of forgings produced, as shown by Lane,[2] who compared the costs of producing a part by forging, and casting. The figures are reproduced in Table 2.

Table 1 Cost of producing drop-forgings: % of total production cost

Material	52
Direct overheads	15
Direct labour	10
Dies	8
Maintenance	4
Stock heating	3
Others	8

Table 2 Comparison of forging and casting production costs

	Sand casting				Drop forging			
Production quantity	100	1000	5 000	10 000	100	1000	5 000	10 000
Blank production. Die, pattern & preparation cost	7·50	0·75	0·17	0·08	19·50	1·95	0·39	0·20
Manufacturing cost	8·30	7·90	7·90	7·90	7·90	5·10	4·85	4·85
Nett cost (dollars)	15·80	8·65	8·07	7·98	27·40	7·05	5·24	5·05
Machining								
Purchased tooling	5·30	0·53	0·13	0·08	5·30	0·53	0·13	0·08
Jigs, fixtures (man-hrs)	0·24	0·02	0·01	0·005	0·24	0·02	0·01	0·005
Labour (man-hrs)	3·60	3·54	3·51	3·51	3·60	3·54	3·51	3·51
Hourly rate	3·80	3·80	3·80	3·80	3·80	3·80	3·80	3·80
Unit tooling and machining cost (dollars)	19·87	14·04	13·47	13·39	19·87	14·04	13·47	13·39
Total unit cost (dollars)	35·67	22·69	21·54	21·37	47·27	21·09	18·71	18·44

The data in Table 2 have been used to draw the curves shown in Fig. 4, from which it is apparent that unless order runs are long and die lives high, the high initial costs of forgings prevent them competing in price with castings. Because of this Hahn and Wood,[7] in an excellent review of the relative merits of forgings and castings, have pointed out that castings are much less costly to redesign at the prototype stage.

Having outlined the present status of forging with conventional plant the remainder of the paper is devoted to a discussion of recent developments and their possible impact in both technical and economic terms.

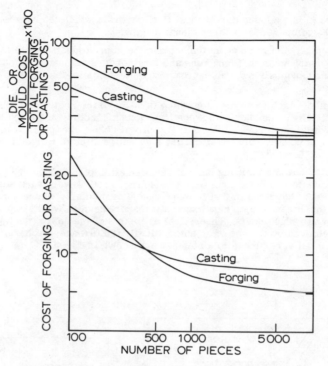

4 Comparative costs for forging and casting production

DEVELOPMENTS IN DROP FORGING

Automation and Mechanical Handling in Drop-Forging

Table 1 showed that labour costs contributed significantly to forging production costs, and this gives drop-forgers an incentive to consider automation as a means of reducing labour and direct overhead costs.

The problem of automation can be approached in two ways. Firstly sophisticated plant can be developed, which is capable of producing a limited range of components at very high production rates. Secondly automatic in-press handling mechanisms may be developed for application to existing plant.

Perhaps the best example of the first approach is the Hatebur automatic forging machine recently installed at a large British forge;[8] in this plant black steel bars up to 20 ft long and between $1\frac{1}{2}$ and $2\frac{3}{8}$ in in diameter, are delivered to an unscrambler, which feeds them one at a time to an electrical resistance heater which heats the bar to forging temperature in one minute. Bars are then transferred to a tunnel-type holding furnace, from where they are passed to the forging machine.

In the forging machine a piece is cropped from the bar and automatically fed through the forging stations, where it is upset, preformed, finish formed, and pierced if necessary. The machine can produce circular components such as gear blanks, flanges, and bearings with tolerances maintained in some cases down to 0·012 in. The forgings are made in enclosed dies without flash or draft, which leads to material savings of about 20% compared with conventional forging.

The high capital cost of such equipment, and the high production rates (up to 4 000 pieces per hour) mean that long runs and large orders are necessary to make the plant viable. Obviously such an approach to automation is only open to the very large-scale forger.

The second approach to automation which is of more interest to the jobbing forger is the possibility of developing automatic in-press handling on conventional forging presses. Whilst such developments are in progress[9,10] the handling equipment at the moment is usually capable of dealing only with a limited range of shapes, principally circular forgings.

Automation of hammer forging has not yet been attempted and indeed presents far more formidable problems than does press forging. However, work study investigations by DFRA[6] have shown that in many cases, particularly where hammer times are short, the use of simple handling and transport devices would improve production rates and reduce costs. Theoretical estimates of the cost reductions which could be achieved by the use of an automatically fed furnace, discharging to a conveyor which delivers pieces to a stamper are shown in Fig. 5.

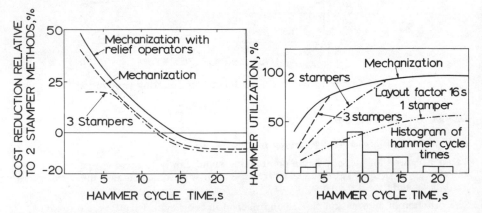

5 Cost savings achievable by mechanical handling in drop forging

The object of such an approach to automation is to reduce the time spent by the stamper in transport handling. The development of suitable furnaces and conveyors is currently being investigated by DFRA.

The extent to which sophisticated programmable robot arms such as the Unimate can be employed in forges is a matter of speculation. The use of a Unimate robot to handle all production operations during forging has been suggested in America,[11] but the life of such delicate equipment in the hostile environment of the forge has not yet been established. However, the gradual introduction of automation and mechanical handling into the drop-forge will undoubtedly occur.

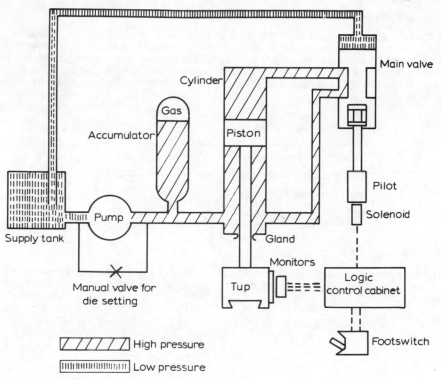

6 Operating principle of the 'Hydrostamp'

Plant Developments

HYDRAULIC HAMMER

For many years hammers and crank-presses have remained almost unchanged in design. Recent developments however, particularly in the field of electrohydraulics, have led to the production of several interesting new forging machines.

One of these is the Hydro Stamp, a hydraulically operated hammer.[12,13] The principle of operation of this machine is shown in Fig. 6. The system is based on the maintenance of a constant hydraulic pressure beneath the piston, and the action of the hammer is controlled by applying or releasing pressure above the piston. A high-speed constant delivery pump supplies fluid at pressure to gas-loaded hydraulic accumulators which maintain fluid pressure on the underside of the hammer piston and deliver fluid, as required, to the upperside of the piston.

The constant pressure lift gives automatic and rapid pickup immediately after a blow has been struck, which results in short die contact time, and minimum heat loss from the forging. This high blow energy and blow rate allows forgings with thin webs to be made in fewer blows than on conventional drop-hammers. The importance of reducing hammer time with respect to the application of mechanical handling has already been emphasised in Fig. 5.

HAMMER-PRESS

A radical departure from conventional forging presses is the recently introduced combined forging hammer-press: this machine is capable of acting as a conventional long-stroke hydraulic press to produce extrusion forgings. In addition it can perform rapid hammering operations such as those required to form flanges on the end of extruded parts. The characteristic features of a 1 000 tonf capacity model are shown in Table 3.

Table 3 Characteristics of 1 000 tonf Hammer-Press

Max. Press capacity	1 000 tonf
Max. Capacity of bottom ejector	300 tonf
Max. Capacity of top ejector	34 tonf
Max. Blow energy as hammer	26 ft-tonf

WEDGE PRESS

The accuracy with which press-forged components can be produced depends in part on the stiffness of the press assembly and the extent to which off-centre loading can be tolerated.

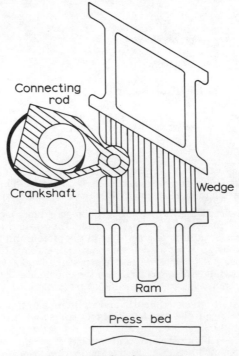

7 Wedge drive for forging press

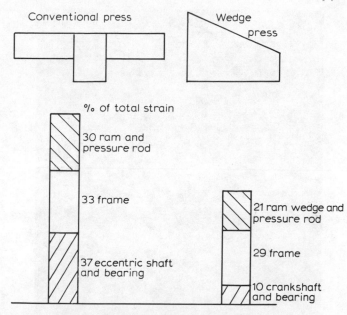

8 Deformation in conventional and wedge-type forging press

A new type of press drive has recently been introduced, as shown in Fig. 7.[16] In this press the forging load is transmitted to the dies by means of a wedge driven by the crank of the press. This design leads to greater rigidity, and the ability to perform off-centre forging with little tilting of the ram. Some of the advantages claimed for the press can be seen in Figs. 8 and 9.

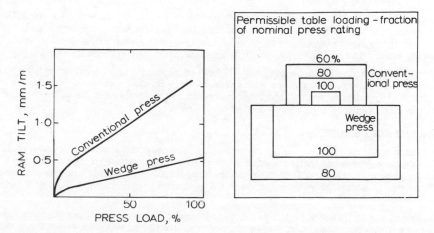

9 Off-centre forging capacity of conventional and wedge-type forging press

10 Multiple-ram forging press

MULTIPLE-RAM PRESSES

Another innovation in press design is the introduction of multiple-ram presses.[17,18] Machines with up to five rams have been built; an example being a press with a 750 tonf capacity clamp ram acting vertically, and four horizontally opposed 150 tonf forging rams. The operation of multiple ram forging is illustrated in Fig. 10.

The use of split dies in these presses allows the production of forgings such as valve bodies, elbows, tees, and crosses with large savings in material, up to 50% having been claimed.[17] In addition significant improvements in properties can be achieved due to the absence of outcropping grain flow at the flash.[17]

'USE' MAKING MACHINE

The importance of preforming for component soundness and material economy has already been stressed. Until recently such preforming was performed under the hammer or on 'reducer-rolls'. The latter, however, are not widely used because of difficulties in designing rolls to produce the required preform shape without lengthy modifications.

Investigations at DFRA have led to the development of a transverse rolling preform machine which produces accurate preforms with simple roll design.[19,20] The principle of operation is shown in Fig. 11.

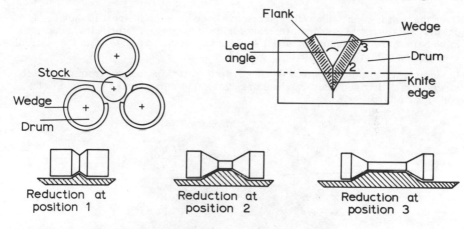

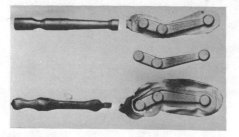

11 DFRA-Redman Preforming Machine

12 Typical flash reduction achieved when using DFRA-Redman Preforming Machine

Numerous trials with the machine have shown that flash wastage on many components at the smaller end of the forging range can be reduced from about 30% to 15% as illustrated in Fig. 12.

FUTURE PLANT AND FORGING PROCESSES

The developments discussed so far have been concerned with improvements in plant used to produce forging by conventional methods.

There are, however, a number of potential developments based on radical departures from conventional forging production. Some of the more promising techniques are now considered.

Forging of Powder-Preforms

Many structural parts made by powder metallurgy techniques have poor physical and mechanical properties. Subsequent forging, however, can produce properties approaching those of conventional wrought components.

Over the past few years therefore, there has been growing interest in the use of powder metallurgy to produce preforms for drop forging. The principal advantage to be gained are substantial material savings and drastic reductions in the machining required on the forging, as shown in Fig. 13.

Development work on this process has covered materials ranging from plain carbon steels to nickel-based alloys, and commercial exploitation can be expected in the very near future.

**13 Forging produced from powder pre-
forms and by conventional means**

Forging of Cast Preforms

Another entirely new approach to the reduction in material wastage is the use of cast preforms for forging. DFRA has investigated the technical feasibility of this method,[19] and has shown that relatively low-grade cast preforms can be upgraded by forging, to produce components with adequate mechanical properties, as shown in Fig. 14.

In America, development has gone even further with the production of the revolu-tionary Autoforge process;[21] in this process molten metal is cast into water-cooled permanent moulds. When the casting is self supporting it is indexed 45°, and air-cooled. The casting is then transferred to a forging station and formed to the final

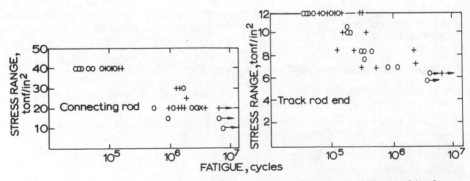

O Forged casting; + Conventional forging; × Commercial forging fully machined

**14 Fatigue test results on forgings produced by conventional means and from forged
castings**

shape under a hydraulic press. The parts are then further cooled before final clipping. An indication of the economic advantages to be gained is given in Table 4.

Table 4 Costs of conventional and Autoforge forgings in brass

	Conventional forging $ per piece	Autoforge forging $ per piece
Material	0·2600	0·1610
Flash	0·0495	—
Reheating and cutting	0·0093	—
Forging labour	0·0054	—
Trimming labour	0·0027	—
Melting	—	0·0270
Labour	—	0·0065
Total cost	0·3269	0·1945
Cost reduction per piece = 40%		

The Petroforge Machine

Some years ago high-energy rate forming (HERF) machines were developed. In these machines the energy for forging is derived from the sudden expansion of compressed gas, which drives a heavy platen holding the forging dies. Such machines, capable of making a forging in a single blow, were heralded as a panacea to all forging problems. However, experience has shown that the low cycling rate, due to the need for hydraulically recompressing the gas, the low die life, and generally high running and maintenance costs, detract seriously from the apparent advantages of the machines.

To overcome the problem of low cycling rate, developments at the University of Birmingham[22] have produced a forging machine in which the energy to drive the platen is derived from the explosion of gaseous fuel, as in the internal combustion engine. This allows blow rates of up to 60 per minute to be achieved. Whilst the production development of the Petroforge has not yet been completed, it does offer an interesting extension to forging plant which may well find application in the future.

PATTERN FOR THE FUTURE

Inevitably, a review of new developments in any industry leads to the temptation to forecast future trends; and if a general pattern can be found linking the developments discussed it suggests that the future in the forging industry will lead to a good deal of rationalization: no longer will the same plant be adapted to make a wide range of forgings; instead, plant will be specifically selected according to the product to which it is most suited. This will lead to specialization in production amongst those forgers, with the requisite plant requirements.

It is possible that for many forgings the press or hammer will be used only for a final sizing operation rather than a means of bulk metal movement, the major shaping having been accomplished in the production of preforms.

For small component preforms, powder metallurgy or the DFRA proforming machine appear to offer the greatest promise, but casting may be more suitable for larger components.

Finally, the introduction of automation and mechanical handling will occur to combat increasing wages and labour shortage.

The future therefore points to fewer, more efficient forges, making components of increased accuracy at a cost competitive with other methods of fabrication.

ACKNOWLEDGEMENTS

The author is grateful to the following companies who supplied illustrations for the paper: GKN Forgings Ltd. and John Shaw and Sons (Salford) Ltd.

REFERENCES

1   K. J. Abbott: *Metal Forming,* 1967, **34**, 1, 19

2   P. H. R. Lane: *Design Engineering Metals Handbook,* 1968, 184

3   Forging Industry Handbook, Forging Industry Association USA

4   T. A. Dean: *Metal Forming,* 1967, **34**, 12, 362

5   T. A. Dean: 7th Int. MTDR Conf. University of Birmingham, Sept. 1966

6   D. A. Laffey: DFRA Rep. S2/68/5

7   E. J. Hahn & R. F. Wood: *Metal Forming,* 1969, **36**, 2, 36

8   Anon: ibid., 1968, **35**, 8, 218

9   J. H. Callaghan & J. Foster: ibid, 1966, **33**, 254, 442

10 Anon: ibid, 1966, **33**, 255, 485

11 Anon: *Light Metals and Metal Industry,* Feb. 1966

12 Anon: *Metal Forming,* 1968, **35**, 6, 172

13 Anon: ibid, 1970, **37**, 4, 110

14 Anon: ibid, 1968, **35**, 2, 52

15 Anon: ibid, 1969, **36**, 10, 288

16 G. Rau: ibid, 1967, **34**, 7, 194

17 J. W. Brougher: Int. Forging Conf. Sheffield, 1967, Sept. 19—21

18 Anon: *Metal Forming,* 1970, **37**, 3, 74

19 A. C. Hobdell & A. Thomas: ibid, 1969, **36**, 1, 17

20 N. S. Boggon: *The Purchasing Journal,* Sept. 1969, 29

21 Anon: *Metal Forming,* 1969, **36**, 7, 196

22 L. T. Chan & S. A. Tobias: 9th Int. M. T. D. R. Conf, 1968, 16—20th Sept, University of Birmingham

CURRENT TECHNIQUES FOR THE PRODUCTION OF CLOSE-TOLERANCE CASTINGS

P. J. F. Horton and D. R. Brammer

Close tolerance, precision, and semiprecision, are all relative terms, and often in the past the foundry has been accused of making wild claims as to the accuracy of specific processes. Generalization is often dangerous since each casting has to be assessed on its own merit. However, in the various references made in the paper, it can be taken that production castings are regularly being made within the values quoted.

In considering the casting processes available for the production of castings of up to about 30 lb, the principal techniques which are applied in the area of close-tolerance castings (often referred to as precision or semiprecision castings) are:

   (i) investment moulding

  (ii) ceramic moulding

 (iii) shell moulding

 (iv) core-sand and greensand moulding.

During the last 25 years the above techniques have been employed or adapted to meet the growing requirement for castings produced to relatively close tolerances, with a high standard of surface finish, and to high standards of inspection and internal soundness.

All the techniques in one form or another are employed in the steel foundries with which the authors are associated, the Weir Group Steel Foundry Division, comprising Catton and Co. Ltd, Osborn-Hadfields Steel Founders Ltd, Osborn Precision Castings Ltd, and E. Jopling and Sons Ltd. For this reason the subject is treated from the steel foundry point of view, although the techniques are applicable to all metals which can be produced in the cast form.

The techniques are listed broadly in the degree of precision which can be attained, and since features such as definition, surface finish, and tolerance fall into more or less the same general classification, not unnaturally, it is fair to say that so does cost. However, it must be borne in mind that the cost of a casting in isolation is not

The scope of this paper, while very broad, endeavours to cover the fundamental features of the four processes described. In addition, some of the significant developments which have led to their rapid growth in the last twenty years are highlighted. The mechanization of each process is discussed, and illustrations are shown of the earliest and the most modern machines available, together with examples of castings produced from them, and the generally accepted tolerances achievable. Particular emphasis is made on how the processes can be, or have been, automated so that they can, or may, become economic for high-volume production. Final emphasis is given on the need for well planned and balanced foundry production units with good control, together with close cooperation with the customer.

The authors are with Osborn-Hadfields Ltd, and the Steel Foundry Division of the Weir Group, respectively

621.74.04

of prime importance, since by employment of one of these processes, with adequate concern for design, much expensive machining or forming is eliminated or reduced, which often serves to substantially reduce the total manufacturing cost.

Figure 1 indicates the saving in machining for a bung-bush produced alternatively as a forging and as a close-tolerance casting, while Fig. 2 shows the difference in producing a small valve from bar stock, and as a shell-moulded casting. The growth of each technique is largely as a result of customer/founder cooperation at the design stage to meet the specific requirement of a particular component. Often a single prototype casting can pave the way for a whole range of components to be produced by a specific process, and in many cases the use of these processes provides the only economic means to produce the requirements of some commercial and military products. The investment casting is usually taken to be one produced by the lost-wax technique and although other ramifications exist, e.g. the frozen mercury process, it is the former which is most significant in the production field.

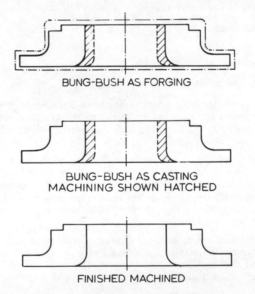

BUNG-BUSH AS FORGING

BUNG-BUSH AS CASTING
MACHINING SHOWN HATCHED

FINISHED MACHINED

1 Bung-bush shown as forging and close-
tolerance casting

There are a number of ceramic-moulding processes, e.g. Osborn-Shaw, Unicast, Avnet-Shaw, and Ceramicast, but the Osborn-Shaw process will be considered since it is employed in daily use in one of the foundries.

The more conventional sand-moulding techniques have been adapted in a number of ways to produce small castings to close tolerances, but generally to supplement castings produced by the first three techniques, and only where due to the low requirement in numbers can the more expensive metal pattern equipment not be economically justified.

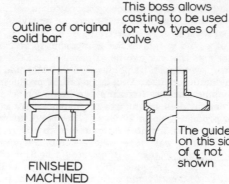

Outline of original solid bar

This boss allows casting to be used for two types of valve

FINISHED MACHINED

The guides on this side of ₵ not shown

AS CAST
Machining allowance shown hatched

a *from bar stock;* b *as shell-moulded casting*

2 Valve

In practice core block moulding in the sodium silicate/CO_2 process and in oilsand have been adopted in the steel foundries principally for the production of prototypes and small series impeller orders. These techniques are often used in combination with some of the benefits afforded by the first three listed.

Finally, with the progress made in high-pressure moulding equipment (jolt and squeeze) for conventional greensand castings, one of the foundries, Catton and Co. Ltd, is in the process of introducing fully automated machine moulding for the production of small- and medium-size steel castings. This technique has been used in some iron foundries during the last few years, but its adoption by the steel foundry has been inhibited due to the complex variables which are encountered, such as short-series production, multiplicity of specifications, and the variation in moulding sand requirements and cooling times with reference to dispersal of liquid metal.

An attempt is made to briefly describe each process together with some of the significant developments which have increased the potential and acceptance of them as an economic reality. Some details of the manner in which the processes are used within the foundries are given, together with a few examples of castings produced.

INVESTMENT CASTING, OR THE LOST-WAX PROCESS

While the investment method of forming materials has developed from an art which can be traced as far back as the Early Egyptian civilization, it is only during the last 30 years that it has substantially developed. The prime catalyst for this rapid development was the demand for aero-engine components during World War II. However, the industrial application for components produced by the technique has grown, and is still growing, as appreciation of its potential for cost saving increases. Following the changing fortunes of the aircraft industry, the search for other markets was stimulated and, combined with substantial technical progress, investment casting is now used in almost all branches of the engineering industry.

The process involves the coating of preformed wax patterns with alternate layers of a fine refractory slip generally applied by dipping or spraying, followed by a stuccoing operation using coarser refractory particles. The number of layers is determined by the geometry, size, and weight of the component to be cast. On establishment of a suitable coating thickness the wax can be eliminated and the mould fired at high temperature before casting, which can be performed directly into the hot mould. One of the foundries, Osborn-Hadfields Steel Founders Ltd, is producing castings by this technique on a relatively small scale. Patterns are formed by the injection of low melting point waxes into metal dies, by the use of purpose-built machines. These machines are capable of producing up to 70 wax forms per hour depending upon the complexity of the die which, where feasible, is designed to eliminate the use of cores. The patterns are then built into a wax 'tree' where suitable feeders and runners are located and wax-welded in place. Figure 3 illustrates a section of the wax room where this operation takes place. The assembly is then inspected and weighed, whereby a suitable factor relative to density can establish the weight to be poured. The wax tree is then dipped to give a primary coat of fine refractory slip which is made from zircon flour (250 mesh) isopropyl silicate and a liquid acid hardener.

The coat is then subjected to a coarser sillimanite material (30 mesh) by a gravity 'raining' technique, or alternatively dipped in a fluidized bed of the material. Drying of the assembly in an ammonia atmosphere requires some ten minutes.

Some two or three coats are applied in this manner, the number is then built to eight or nine by a similar, but coarser slurry, and with alternate layers of molochite, again applied by means of a fluidized bed. The coated assembly and the initial wax tree are illustrated in Fig. 4. Wax elimination is achieved by use of a steam autoclave, using superheated steam at 150°C, and subsequent to this the mould is allowed to cool. The resulting ceramic shell is then fired for two hours at 950°C in a muffle furnace, from which the moulds can be removed hot and immediately clamped to one of a series of small indirect arc furnaces. The moulds are poured by inversion of the furnace, the technique being known as the Durville system. The furnaces utilize premelted bar stock of certified analysis and produce a wide variety of specifications which can be melted under an argon atmosphere.

3 View of wax pattern room

4 Wax tree before and after investment

Figure 5 shows a typical investment casting produced by the process in large numbers. The casting is used in a precombustion chamber of a diesel engine and cast in a high-nickel alloy. It can be seen that many machining operations have been eliminated, and it is difficult to envisage its production by any other method without redesign.

5 Typical lost-wax casting ×2/3

Advantages of the process

The advantages afforded by the process are numerous, since close dimension tolerances within the practical range of ±0·005 in/in can be achieved, and hence castings can be produced which require minimum machining in critical areas. Often parts require no machining and can be used as cast or heat-treated. The as-cast surface finish is excellent, and on steel falls generally in the range 60—120 μin $\sqrt{\text{mean}^2}$. The process has an inherent advantage in that no mould joint or parting line is necessary to remove the pattern, and accordingly the tolerances can be maintained evenly in three directions at right angles. The process also facilitates the production of components in alloys which are virtually unmachineable or relatively difficult to machine. Cleanliness and internal soundness are also features of the process so necessary to the rigorous inspection standards to which many castings are produced.

Development

The most significant change in the process has been the almost universal adoption of the ceramic-shell technique as opposed to the former block-mould technique in which after the initial dipcoats a refractory slurry was poured around the investment to produce a solid mould. The shell technique has prevented wastage of expensive binder material and has much improved the ease of wax elimination, since in the former technique the slow rate of heat transfer through the refractory mass made this a difficult and time-consuming operation.

The development of the fluidized bed for applying the stuccoing materials has improved the coating operation both in uniformity and speed, and the use of the chemical drying system has drastically shortened the time required to produce a mould.

Considerable study has led to the development of new waxes having different properties, such as surface texture and melting point. The latter is important since unless
progressive elimination of wax from the downgate to mould can be achieved, cracking
of the ceramic shell is often experienced. Filled waxes also contribute to the improvement of mould surfaces which in turn are reflected in castings. The use of the
steam autoclave has improved the efficiency of wax elimination and permitted a high
level of wax recovery and re-use, with attendent economy. However, the wax is only
used to form runners and feeders, due to possible ash content spoiling the mould
surface. The future of the process looks quite bright providing the relatively high
costs can be reduced principally in the utilization of labour.

To this end some fully- and semi-automated plants have been installed. A new installation[1] by GEC Elliott Precision Control at the works of Deritend Precision
Castings Limited is capable of producing 144 six-coat investments within one eight-
hour shift using only one operator. Reference has also been made to a new technique[2]
where rapid formation of the mould is achieved by chemical methods and a six-coat
investment can be prepared in a matter of a few minutes when coupled with shock
dewaxing.

Alternative to the Durville system for pouring is the 'bottom-pour' induction-melting
technique.[3] In this a high-frequency induction coil is used to promote melting in a
preformed crucible which has a small hole in the bottom covered by a plug forming
part of the charge. On melting, the plug can be designed to melt at a specified temperature and so fill a mould situated beneath it. Individual small melts can be produced in a matter of minutes. It is thus feasible that with the combination of a fully
automated investment plant and this principle of melting that the process can be fully
integrated and automated as far as the stripping of the casting from the mould.

It is understood that turbine blades have been manufactured by the investment technique using a fully integrated line which encompasses automatic X-ray equipment
for each component.

CERAMIC MOULDING (OSBORN-SHAW PROCESS)

The Osborn-Shaw process is a ceramic-mould investment technique employing re-
usable master patterns in place of the expendable wax patterns utilized in the lost-
wax technique. The first stage in the process is the manufacture of the master pattern, preferably in brass, bronze, steel, or resin for dimensional stability. Wood can
be used, but it tends to change dimensions due to absorption of moisture.

The mould material is poured by the operator in the form of a slurry on to a prepared pattern treated with a parting agent. The gelling action of the slurry is so controlled that within a matter of seconds the slurry changes to a tough rubbery gel
which eventually solidifies. The mould is stripped from the pattern while in this
pliable condition, making possible the use of patterns with little or no moulding taper.
Immediately the moulds have been removed from the pattern they are flamed to
ensure rapid removal of alcohol. This flaming causes the mould to craze-crack
throughout its mass producing high permeability and partial immunity to thermal
shock. Subsequently the moulds are closed and fired at high temperature to further
strengthen the bond and ensure that it is strong, inert, gas free, and erosion resistant.
A variety of moulding materials are used which are basically graded alumino-sili-
cate, a liquid binder based on ethyl silicate, and a gelling agent, isopropyl alcohol.
The gelling, or hydrolysis, of the ethyl silicate is controlled by an acid catalyst, and
the reaction results in the precipitation of silica around the grains of refractory to

form a bond. The basic mix utilizes natural refractory, e.g. sillimanite (60AL-40Si), for the facing mix, and a cheaper molochite as backing material. In order to reduce costs, synthetic alumina silicates can be used when a single refractory mix is used. However, the substitution of sillimanite results in inferior surface finish, and lowering the ethyl silicate/isopropyl-alcohol ratio gives a weaker bond and some loss of· dimensional accuracy.

The fired moulds, after cooling, are cored and closed, then held together in a clamping fixture. The joint can be sealed with a slurry of molochite, a process known as 'luting'. After closing the mould is fired at 1 000°C to drive off combined moisture, and then poured while still hot. Alternatively the mould halves can be fired separately, cored, closed by clamping, and poured with the clamps in position. The latter method gives a little better control of dimensional variation across the joint.

Advantages of the process

Unlike the investment technique, the mould has a parting line to permit pattern removal, and this slightly reduces the tolerances which can be held at right angles to the joint. Tolerances from ±0·005 to ±0·015in/in are being achieved dependent on section size and configuration. Very thin sections can be run, with practical minimum of 0·06in on certain designs. The surface finish produced in steel is good, and ranges from 70—120 in. The process is suited to castings of high complexity and definition since faithful registration of pattern detail is achieved. Metal sections are unusually clean due to an inert mould, and high permeability ensures absence of airlocks.

These attributes facilitate the production of castings to class 1 standards of inspection and radiographic soundness. Figure 6 shows a casting produced for aero-engines to AID standards. The component is a prototype casting produced by a combination of casting and fabrication. The extent of machining illustrates the necessity for castings which are not scrapped at a late stage in forming. This photograph illustrates the prototype development possible by this process within short delivery times by proper customer and founder cooperation. The process has been used successfully for this type of component, and in addition for the manufacture of various types of die where final polishing only is necessary.

6 Osborn-Shaw casting for an aero-
  engine

Development

Not a great deal has been done to mechanize the process, since in the group foundries it is regarded as more suited to small-series and prototype production. However, simple mechanical application can permit large numbers of moulds to be produced. Figure 7 shows such a mechanical device which worked in pairs, and was used for the production of some 3 000 golf club heads per week. The process lends itself to stack moulding with resultant economy in refractory cost. Costs are also reduced by the use of composite moulds with a fine refractory facing and metal or CO_2 silica sand backing. For backing-up techniques the materials can be reclaimed and re-used. Castings from 2—3 tons in weight have been reported in both the USA and Japan by use of suitable backing materials.

Dual self-proportioning mixers for slurry preparation and machines similar in principle to the one illustrated in Fig. 7 have assisted in development of the technique, but the fact that shell moulding is a cheaper method for large-scale production has limited the sphere of activity for this ceramic process. However, since the tolerances are somewhat intermediate between the shell and investment techniques, much wider application is still quite feasible.

7 **Mechanical device for Osborn-Shaw mould production**

SHELL MOULDING

This originated in Germany and was known as the 'C Process', or 'Croning Process'. After World War II the process was taken up both in the USA and the UK, although initially the Americans made greater use of it. Development in the UK was somewhat slower, and only really commenced in about 1952 or 1953.

The process involves the manufacture of a thin-walled sand mould of controlled thickness, (0·25—0·75 in) from a heated metal pattern plate (200—240°C). The formation of the shell is brought about by 'dumping', or blowing a resin-coated sand mixture, which is usually silica and a two-stage phenolic resin, on to the heated pattern plate. This is rendered thermosetting on contact with heat by hexamethylenetetramine incorporated in the mix, thus allowing the formation of a rigid shell mould. After curing in an oven the mould is mechanically stripped from the pattern, cored, closed, and cast. In both shell moulding and shell coremaking, which use the same technique, the thickness of the mould, or core, is controlled by the time, 'investment time', the resin-coated sand is in contact with the pattern or corebox. Excess sand is then drained away. Figure 8 shows a typical mould before and after the closing operation.

8 Typical shell mould

Development

A variety of shell-moulding machines are used to suit varying requirements of rate of production, thickness of shell, and size of pattern plate. Early shell-mould machines use the 'dump box' principle where a 'box' of sand is invested onto a heated pattern plate. The whole is re-inverted, allowing the uncured sand to fall back into the box. The pattern is moved back to the heat source, and the thin coating of sand cures when it can be ejected by suitably placed ejector pins. After ejection the two halves of the mould can be cored and closed by pressure, either in the form of a 'vacuum closer' or a 'pin closer'. The pressure is maintained for the time that a resin glue takes to set after application to the joint line of the two mould halves.

The trend in the mechanization of shell moulding has been a logical progression from wholly manually operated machines to the fully automatic repeat-cycling moulding and coremaking machines currently available.

Figure 9 shows one of the early machines which, in spite of mechanical assistance on the sand dump and sand dump return, was very slow and tedious. It was capable of producing 9–12 moulds per hour, $\frac{7}{16}$–$\frac{9}{16}$ in thick in a 4·8% resin sand.

Figure 10 shows a single-station repeat- or single-cycle automatic moulding machine which has been successfully used in many foundries. It will produce between 25 and 30 moulds per hour, $\frac{7}{16}$–$\frac{9}{16}$ in thick in a 4·8% resin sand. On repeat cycling the operator only removes the mould from the machine, leaving the machine free to commence and complete the next cycle unattended. In some cases the mould removal is mechanized and the mould is presented to the operator away from the machine, which then automatically commences the next cycle. This sequence enables the operator to core and close the mould within the cycle of the machine.

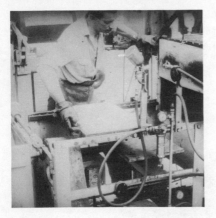

9 Early shell-moulding machine

10 Automatic shell-moulding machine

The ancilliary equipment to this type of machine is as important as the machine itself, otherwise the closing operation is likely to be extended outside the cycle of the machine. The operator will then slow down the machine to enable him to complete the closing operation. Thus the development of shell and mould handling devices, fully mechanized closing operations, and faster curing resin glues have been very important. This may sound like overstating the obvious, but all too often the authors have seen this type of machine operating well below optimum output because of this problem. Figure 11 shows a group of castings in different material specifications produced in large quantities from this type of machine.

11 Shell-moulded castings

One of the inherent problems in achieving high outputs from shell-moulding or core-making machines is the investment and cure time. Given optimum heating conditions and a specific resin content these cannot be speeded up unless there is a major change in resin technology. The only other way to maximize production is to ensure that there is a minimum of delay between each machine operation and machine cycle. Many of the currently available single-station machines have achieved these conditions, and in terms of output there is little to choose between them. However, by designing machines with independent sequencing of multipattern or core box set-ups, utilizing common sand dump or blow cure and ejection facilities, higher output per man/machine can be achieved. There are many ways of doing this, such as a four-station rotary machine with arms carrying patterns or coreboxes which are indexed through separate investment cure and ejection stations.

Figure 12 shows part of a multistation machine[4] which is in current use in one of the Group Foundries. The illustration shows the two high deck principles used. The machine has nine moulding frames, each of which is capable of housing up to four patterns, depending on size. The principle is simply a movement of the plates loop fashion. Movement around the ends of the 'loop' is provided by the carrier arms and frame which can be seen in the illustration.

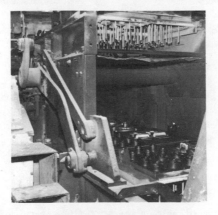

**12 Multistation automatic shell-
moulding machine**

By using a common dump station, oven, ejection and mould removal, this motion provides three frames undergoing investment, and four undergoing cure. This gives an output of up to 1 400 closed moulds per 8-hour working shift, $7/_{16}$–$9/_{16}$in thick in 4·8% resin sand. By using a preheat station, pattern changing is achieved in about 20 seconds within the machine cycle. Together with the 9 pattern frames, this feature ensures the machine is capable of producing small-batch production of say 50—100 shells, together with long runs.

The type of casting currently being produced on this machine can be seen in Fig. 13. The smaller casting weighing 22 oz is made in multiples of 1 000. The larger casting weighing 20lbs is made in batches of 50—100. These can be made simultaneously on the machine.

Figure 14 shows a repeat cycling automatic core blowing machine. This machine ejects the finished cores on to the belt conveyor which delivers them into a storage bin and will continuously produce cores $4^{1}/_{4}$in o.d. $3/_{4}$in section from a multi-gang

13 Shell-moulded castings

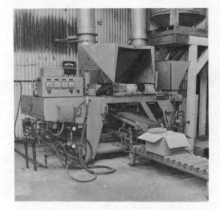

14 Automatic shell core machine

box set-up at the rate of 700/h. It will operate virtually unattended, leaving the operator free to use other machines, etc., within the vicinity. Other machines also incorporate devices for 'rocking' the core box to and fro within the machine cycle to
ensure surplus sand-drain throughout the inside core profile.

Parallel with machine development have been the vast improvements in materials,
the most important of which is the moulding material. The original mixture was
suitably graded silica sand, mixed dry, with a powdered phenolic resin. This proved
to have many disadvantages:

    (i) mixing was a dusty operation

    (ii) excess resin had to be used

    (iii) segregation of resin took place

    (iv) control of the dust by oil lowered the shell strength.

Modern sands are precoated, which gives far better control, and modern resin technology[8] has given higher-strength shells where required, virtual elimination of pin-
holding due to evolution of nitrogen, and generally specific coated sands to meet certain duties.

Advantages and tolerances

Foundry method and feeding techniques have been developed specifically for shell,
and generally the process occupies a place midway between investment and greensand castings. These are the advantages of the technique:

    (i) closer tolerances. Generally this can be stated as: up to 2 ± 0·015in, 2—4 ±
       0·030in, then 0·004in for each additional inch

    (ii) mould taper reduced

    (iii) thinner wall sections and intricate coring

    (iv) good surface finish and repeatability

    (v) good collapsability of the mould

    (vi) use of semiskilled labour.

The advanced machinery and techniques described enable the well equipped foundry to mass- or batch-produce close-tolerance high-definition castings with excellent repeatability. The total tonnage of the group of foundries is over 200 tons per week of shell-moulded castings, comprising 50 000—100 000 pieces in up to 100 different steel specifications, although predominant production is made in about twenty specifications. The modern machinery described can also be developed into purpose-built integrated flow lines for the mass production of specialized products. This is particularly true of the automobile industry making iron castings in the USA, and to a lesser degree in the UK, where fully mechanized moulding and metal-pouring lines are used. This technique could be developed for high-volume mass production of steel castings in this country, and used to give considerable economies over previous methods of production; it would enable the foundry to compete better with existing metal-forming processes.

SAND MOULDING

As stated, some conventional sand-moulding techniques have been adapted to produce close-tolerance small castings, and it is felt that two of these are worthy of mention.

CO_2 block moulding

This technique is adapted from the widely used CO_2 sodium silicate process normally applied to medium and large castings. In order to take its place in the production of close-tolerance castings, special sand mixes have been devised to meet the requirements of accuracy and good surface finish.

Refractory facing of very fine silica sand (AFS no.100—150) or zircon is used with a backing of coarser silica, both mixes being bonded with 6% sodium silicate and hardened by the passage of CO_2. The facing is usually some 0·5 in thick, and gassing the mould only requires some two or three minutes. Mould permeability is low and artificial venting is necessary; cores and moulds can be made by hand ramming or blowing techniques in the conventional manner. The moulded surface is protected from friability by the use of a spirit based resin spray, and patterns are produced in metal resin or wood, depending on the surface finish or accuracy desired, and also with regard to the number required to be produced from the equipment.

The process can produce surface finishes and dimensional accuracies, though not generally as good as with the Osborn-Shaw process, still of the order of ± 0·015in/in. The process is suited to one-off production or to series production. However, some disadvantages exist since the refractory is difficult to strip and does not break down easily and production rates are slow.

A similar technique using oils, based on linseed oil, in place of the silicate bond is used for small run impeller and diffuser production. A typical impeller is shown in Fig.15. Collapsibility of the poured mould is improved but production cost increased due to the necessity to bake the moulds at about 200°C.

The two techniques described can often best be utilized when used in composite moulds. Combinations of Osborn-Shaw shell moulding and block moulding can be used to exploit the advantages of each process. For example a ceramic core can be used in a block mould where gas from a normal core could cause local blowing or unsoundness; shell cores can be used in CO_2 moulds since they give better breakdown and can be produced faster than CO_2 cores. In this way the specific attributes of each process can be put to their best economic advantage.

15 Block mould Osborn-Shaw
impeller

Greensand moulding

As mentioned earlier the application of high-pressure jolt and squeeze moulding
(100–400 lb/in^2) to steel castings has been inhibited due to the complex variables
which must be controlled and the economic considerations of applying high capital
cost plant to short-series production. The subject is too wide to cover in a paper
of this length, but it should be noted that in many iron foundries where this type of
plant has been installed, considerable improvements in tolerance and finish have
been experienced. A particular feature has been the reproducibility of casting
weights, which indicate a much more volume stable mould.

Tolerances of ± 0·020in/in have been claimed in some iron foundries, but at the
moment the authors do not wish to make any claims for steel. However, it is not
unreasonable to assume that better tolerances will be achieved, and that reduction
in dressing costs and improved reproduction of the pattern detail will be experienced.

A further automatic system producing close-tolerance castings in greensand is the
Disamatic unit.[6] This is a fully automatic plant producing boxless moulds, which are
blown in a cavity, the ends of which form the pattern detail. After blowing, the mould
compacts are moved forward in linear fashion to form a row of closed moulds each
in contact with its neighbour. The moulds are extremely rigid and volume stable, and
with due attention to sand control claims of ± 0·005in/in are made.

Finishing

While the paper is not intended to cover the dressing or finishing aspect of these
processes, it is normally performed by conventional techniques. However, it is essential to note that great care is exercised in order that the benefits derived from the
moulding technique are not impaired by subsequent handling and processing of the
castings. Such features as very fine abrasives, and atmosphere-controlled heat-
treatment furnaces are essential to the preservation of detail achieved in moulding.

Since it is impossible to guarantee the soundness of any casting unless it has been
X-rayed, the latest non-destructive testing techniques must also be applied. In this

way the high-quality standards to which this type of casting is required can be checked and maintained. In future consideration it is feasible that X-ray fluoroscopy[7] will assist in the development and improvement of quality castings by giving more precise understanding of metal flow in relation to the elimination of casting defects.

CONCLUSIONS

Generally speaking, ceramic moulding as used in the Osborn-Shaw process and CO_2 block moulding can only be regarded as suitable for prototype development, and small-batch production. The major growth areas have been in lost wax and shell mould.

The authors would emphasise that the sophisticated plant and techniques outlined in this paper, if purchased and used without proper thought, will yield little or nothing. The desired result must be a balanced production unit[8] backed by effective management using the best available control and production techniques to achieve planned profits. In this way competitive mass production can be achieved which will best serve the customer and foundry producer.

Only by selling the benefits of the techniques outlined, and thus breaking down existing prejudice against the use of castings, can the modern foundry competitively enter into fields traditionally dominated by other metal-forming processes. By close co-operation with the customer, using value analysis type techniques and combining these with new developments within the process discussed, further overall cost savings can be achieved.

ACKNOWLEDGMENTS

The authors wish to thank the Directors of the Weir Group Steel Foundry Division for permission to publish this paper, and also customers, for their agreement to publish photographs of the various castings.

REFERENCES

1   A. W. Astrop: *Machinery and Production Engineering*, 6 May 1970, 713—716

2   'A lost-wax mould every 60 seconds?', *Foundry Trade Journal*, 1970, **128**, 2772, 111—115

3   E. B. Gosling: 'Induction melting for precision investment casting', Proc. 1st world conf. on investment casting, 1966, paper **29**, 1—5

4   J. Fallows and J. Worthington: *The British Foundryman*, 1969, **62**, 7, 260—272

5   F. LeServe: *The British Foundryman*, 1969, **62**, 12, 455—457

6   A. R. Parkes: 'Moulding equipment for small- and medium-size steel castings', BSCRA Conf. 'Plant engineering in steel foundries', 1965, paper 2, 1—31

7   H. T. Hall: *BSCRA Journal*, 1968, 99, 43—54

8   J. H. Osborn *et al.*: *The British Foundryman*, 1958, **51**, 2, 64—76

MACHINING

J. O. Cookson and G. Sweeney

There are over one million machine tools in current use in Great Britain, and about eighty thousand of these are being replaced every year; metal-cutting machine tools hold 85% of this market, metal-forming machines[1] hold 15%; furthermore, 90% of the workpieces undergoing forming operations require subsequent machining by a metal-cutting machine tool. From the facts, it is obvious that metal-cutting machines dominate the market at present.

However, the manufacturers of metal-cutting machine tools are not complacent, since they wish to increase their proportion of the machine-tool market both at home and abroad; to achieve this objective, metal-cutting machine tools must be developed to give increased output with reduced material wastage, to accommodate greater ranges of workpiece materials, and to offset future shortages of skilled machine-tool operators by including more automatic-control facilities.

MACHINE-TOOL DESIGN

Machine tools are made from structures upon which various parts move; there are mechanisms, sources of power, and control systems. To satisfy the conditions of increased production with reduced material wastage, machine tools must be capable of accommodating greater machining powers to give larger metal-removal rates, while reducing uncontrolled movements between tools and workpieces; these requirements lead to stringent design conditions and, almost inevitably, computer-aided design procedures are being used to optimize the many variables involved.

Machine-tool structures must be stiff to transmit greater machining powers and to reduce unwanted tool/workpiece deflections. Not only must machine-tool structures be stiff enough to resist the application of steady machining forces, they must also be

It is likely that future metalworking machines will have to meet requirements of increased production and reduced material wastage, while being able to accommodate a wide range of workpiece materials; furthermore, it is likely that there will be a shortage of skilled machine operators. Metal-cutting machine tools are utilizing a variety of approaches to satisfy these requirements. Stricter machine-tool design procedures are being adopted with respect to structures, bearings, gearboxes, and transmissions; better machine-tool utilization is being vigorously followed, and substantial efforts are being directed towards automatic machine loading and unloading, work transfer, inspection, and assembly. Most of the research and development work which is being carried out at present is consistent with the concept of computer-controlled, integrated manufacturing units, and a number of these units are already available commercially. New machining processes and techniques, e.g. electrodischarge machining, and electrochemical machining, are also being developed to supplement more traditional processes. These approaches are described in the text, and, from the descriptions, it is evident that the metal-cutting machine-tool industry is progressive and well equipped to move into the future.

Both authors are with MTIRA

621.91

stiff enough to resist the application of vibratory forces; in other words, structures must be stiff both statically and dynamically. Static stiffness depends entirely upon the rigidity of the structure, whereas dynamic stiffness is a function of the rigidity of the structure and of the amount of damping (ability to dissipate vibrational energy) in the structure. Computer-aided design procedures are available at MTIRA to predict static stiffness of structures and certain vibratory characteristics; however, they do not predict dynamic stiffness, as it is not possible to supply practical information with respect to structural damping at present, but research investigations are being carried out to rectify this situation. The dynamic stiffnesses of many machine-tool structures can be increased significantly by employing vibration absorbers as appropriate; vibration absorbers must be tuned to the vibrational characteristics of the machine-tool structure upon which they are to be employed; the tuning procedure is complicated, but computer-aided design programs are available at MTIRA to simplify the process.

The ability of any machine tool to reduce the influence of vibrational energy without the assistance of vibrational absorbers, depends largely upon the energy-absorbing properties of its slideways, bearings, and joint faces, as these components contribute over 90% of the energy-absorbing capabilities of any machine tool. Consequently, a number of research investigations are being carried out to utilize joints and bearings more efficiently as major and controlled sources of machine-tool damping; an attempt is being made to improve and control joint-face damping by inserting polymer materials or viscous oils between the joint faces; furthermore although it is not possible to predict accurately the amount of damping associated with most designs of bearings and slideways, hydrostatic bearings are exceptions to this, and it may be possible to insert predetermined amounts of damping into machine-tool structures in future by utilizing hydrostatic bearings. From the efforts being made at present, it is hoped that in the not-too-distant future it will be possible to design metal-cutting machine tools which are chatter-free.

The availability of efficient design procedures has assisted the development of machine tools of modular constructions which must be both light and rigid; of course modular construction of machine tools, an example of which is shown in Fig. 1, allows interchangeability of machine-tool components with resulting improvements in choice of operating configurations.

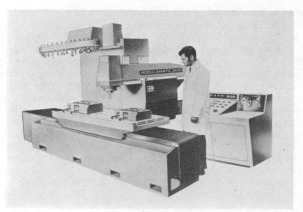

1 Machine tool of modular construction

Cast-iron machine-tool structures are most popular at present, although steel fabrications, which are inherently stiffer, are also used extensively, particularly for special-purpose machines; however, steel fabrications have a greater tendency to creep than cast iron, and such fabrications normally employ cast-iron slideways to reduce the effects of creep. Machine-tool manufacturers are also exploring the use of other materials for machine tools, and plastics are already being used extensively for machine-tool guards and covers.

It is often forgotten that foundations provide substantial amounts of stiffness and damping to machine-tool assemblies, and that inferior machine-tool performances can often be traced to foundations. However, efficient utilization of foundations is now possible by employing the design procedures which are available at MTIRA.

Machine-tool spindles, as well as structures, must be stiff, both statically and dynamically, to transmit large values of machining power; furthermore they must be free-running and capable of accommodating wide ranges of speed and load; the latter requirement will become increasingly important as machine tools are called upon to machine wider ranges of workpiece materials. Again, computer-aided design programs are desirable to design spindles efficiently, and programs for the design of spindles held between two bearings are available from MTIRA.

The characteristics of spindle bearings are also important to machine-tool performance. Hydrodynamic bearings, ball bearings, and roller bearings are popular, and are used extensively by machine-tool manufacturers; however, it is difficult to design any of the preceding bearings with predictable values of performance. Hydrostatic bearings are predictable in the design stages and are being increasingly used by manufacturers. Computer-aided design procedures which are capable of predicting the characteristics of complicated hydrostatic bearing and slideway configurations have been developed and are available at MTIRA.

Computer programs are also available to design stiff, efficient drive systems. Recently variable-speed electric drives, such as electrohydraulic motors, printed motors, etc. have been making significant inroads into the market of hydraulic motors with respect to infeed systems, and this trend is expected to continue. Although the combination of capital cost and maintenance cost is similar for both hydraulic and electric motors, the latter require significantly less maintenance effort than the former, this desirable feature being of major importance with numerically controlled machine tools which cannot tolerate numerous breakdowns. In future, linear electric pulse motors may even eliminate leadscrews. The intelligent employment of gearboxes is obviously critical to most drive systems, and computer programs are available at MTIRA to optimize the selections of gears and gearbox layouts; design procedures are also available to optimize the torsional rigidities and dynamic characteristics of gearboxes, and thereby ensure stiff, positive transmissions for machine tools.

The performance of any well designed drive system is jeopardized by stick-slip and slideway inaccuracies. A considerable amount of work is being undertaken to reduce the possibility of stick-slip in slideways; hardened slideways are employed, and friction is reduced by employing p.t.f.e. and phenolic resin on slideway faces; stick-slip is also reduced on slideways by using ball bearings, roller bearings, hydrostatic bearings, and aerostatic bearings, where applicable. Plain slideways are notorious with respect to stick-slip but recent work has shown that stick-slip can be reduced significantly by employing polar additives in plain slideway oils. The accuracy of assembly of slideways has been greatly assisted recently by the advent of laser measurement techniques, such techniques being supplied as a service by MTIRA to its member firms.

It is anticipated that many individual machine-tool design programs will be integrated into a single suite of computer programs, by means of which computer-aided design of complete machine tools, including structures, transmissions, bearings, etc. will be carried out. In fact the first steps to provide such an integrated procedure are already under way.

It is realized that machine tools which are technically sound may not sell in competitive markets unless they are also functionally correct, that is their controls, instructions, etc. are positioned sensibly, and unless they are visually correct, this latter factor often being accounted for by the sensible employment of colour. Consequently a substantial amount of research and development is being carried out in the fields of ergonomics and industrial design..

It is difficult to illustrate satisfactorily the types of advantages obtained from the employment of modern design procedures, as each of the aspects so far described would require extensive and individual treatment; however, Figs. 2 and 3 should suffice as examples of the modern approach to machine-tool design and to show the significant strides which have been made in recent years.

early design   *modern design*

2 Design developments in milling machines in recent years

Higher metal-removal rates inevitably mean the transmission of more power to the cutting tool; the ability of cutting-tool materials to accept increased power is a major limiting factor. Fig. 4[1] shows the improvements in allowable cutting speeds, and hence metal-removal rates, which have developed with the introduction of different types of tool materials. However, the actual employment of tool materials by machine-tool users is not so tidy as Fig. 4 implies; high-speed tools and cutters, both with and without the employment of replaceable inserts, are still being developed[2] and are used extensively, although tungsten carbide tools are making increasing inroads into the market; unfortunately their acceptance by the market is slower than would be expected from their cutting potential, as they are brittle and demand stiff machine tools for satisfactory performance without breakage. The acceptance of carbide hobs should be more rapid as hobbing machines are recognized as possessing sufficient rigidity to utilize carbide hobs effectively; there is some controversy with respect to the efficiency of solid carbide hobs as against carbide inserts, since the former ensure higher production rates, but cost more than the latter. Other tool materials are being developed continuously to give larger metal-removal rates than

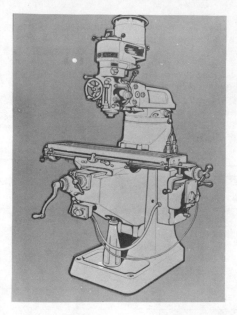

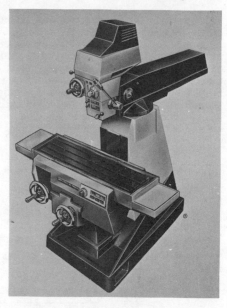

early design

modern design

3 Design developments in drilling machines in recent years

PERMISSIBLE CUTTING SPEED (FOR 125 000lb/in² UTS STEEL) ft/min

Carbon tool steel

High tool steel

Cast non-ferrous

Sintered carbide (steel-cutting type)

Cermet

Ceramic

AF experimental (estimated)

Permissible speed

Permissible UTS

PERMISSIBLE ULTIMATE TENSILE STRENGTH (FOR CUTTING SPEED OF 100 ft/min), lb/in²

YEAR OF INTRODUCTION TO PRACTICE

4 Improvements instigated by different tool materials

those available at present; titanium carbide, which is inherently brittle, is giving excellent results of tool life and metal-removal rate when a thin layer of this material is applied to a tough, cemented-carbide core. In spite of associated large rates of metal removal, the employment of ceramic tools is not widespread, as these tools are very brittle; for example, ceramic inserts obtained a share of only 2% of the tool insert market in 1968.[3] The utilization of increased machining powers to give larger metal-removal rates is particularly evident with grinding, as shown by Fig. 5.[1] Grinding wheels are being developed continuously to accommodate greater machining powers, recent developments including polyurethane-bonded wheels, boron-nitride grits, and the more widespread application of diamond wheels.

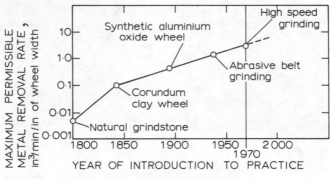

5 Improvements in precision grinding of steel

Efficient machine-tool design is not the most influential factor of increased production; far greater increases of production are possible by proper control and utilization of machine tools, and current attitudes to these factors in the metal-cutting machine-tool industry will now be described.

CONTROL AND UTILIZATION OF MACHINE TOOLS

Machine-tool manufacturers and machine-tool users are making determined efforts to automate and fully utilize metal-cutting machine tools, both to increase production and to counter the future shortage of skilled machine-tool operators.

Table 1[4] shows machine-tool activity figures for general-purpose machine tools, based upon observations in a number of workshops.

It is evident from Table 1 that a large amount of production time is wasted by setting tools upon the machine; consequently techniques of setting tools off the machine have been developed, thereby giving minimum interruption to the machining process; occasionally, toolsetting machines are required. With the employment of interchangeable tools, automatic changing of preset tools becomes an attractive production philosophy.

Automatic control of machine tools is not a new concept as it has been in operation, in some form or another, for many years; at present, control techniques are being developed rapidly and there is no reason to doubt that the rate of development will

Table 1   Machine-tool activity for general-purpose machine-tools,%

	Milling machines	Centre lathes	Turret lathes	Planing machines	Drilling machines	Capstan lathes
a	9·1	7·4	7·3	9·3	16·9	7·7
b	16·2	17·9	16·0	12·0	12·1	16·7
c	1·3	2·1	1·2	1·2	1·1	1·3
d	0·7	0·3	1·1	0·7	1·1	1·2
e	2·8	6·0	4·2	2·7	1·2	3·6
f	24·2	25·4	27·8	26·8	32·5	32·0
g	45·7	40·9	42·4	47·3	35·1	37·5
	100·0	100·0	100·0	100·0	100·0	100·0
h	84·0	76·8	82·9	89·2	69·2	79·8
i	1 867	1 638	1 353	1 241	1 551	1 317

	Horizontal boring machines	Vertical boring machines	Cylindrical grinding machines	Surface-grinding machines	Total
a	12·7	12·3	18·1	14·4	10·7
b	17·9	14·8	11·2	11·9	15·1
c	1·4	1·0	2·8	1·0	1·4
d	0·7	0·4	0·4	0·6	0·8
e	2·7	5·6	7·5	6·4	3·9
f	28·6	24·3	15·0	21·0	26·7
g	36·0	41·1	45·0	44·7	41·4
	100·0	100·0	100·0	100·0	100·0
h	80·7	88·8	64·3	68·7	78·7
i	998	580	787	709	12 041

a	Loading and unloading
b	Idle, loaded, operator absent
c	Idle, operator receiving instructions
d	Miscellaneous
e	Gauging
f	Setting and handling
g	Cutting
h	Proportion of machine time usefully employed
i	Total number of observations

continue into the foreseeable future; the advantages of automatic control become apparent from the production time lost due to machine-tool operators which is shown in Table 1. A number of methods are available for controlling machine tools, including:

   (i)   plugboard control

  (ii)   point-to-point tape control

 (iii)   point-to-point straight line tape control

 (iv)   point-to-point straight line tape control combined with contouring by traces

  (v)   continuous-path contouring by tape

 (vi)   continuous-path with adaptive control

(vii)   direct computer control.

Machine tools can be controlled mechanically by means of cams and linkages, but mechanical control is very slow and has been replaced to a large extent by plugboard control. With plugboard control, wires are conducted from the machine tool to the control board, and cutting speeds and feeds are selected by electrical circuit modifications; if switches are used instead of plugs to modify the circuits the technique is known as sequential control.

The rapid advancement of machine-tool control has been due to the application of numerical control procedures, and an example of a numerically controlled machine tool is shown in Fig. 6. Numerical control allows the positions and velocities of machine-tool units to be planned by digital counting techniques; consequently control instructions are determined in advance, punched upon control tapes, and converted into physical actions by suitable electrical hardware. Numerical control of machine tools increases the time spent cutting metal, and is very flexible; by simply altering the input data tape, the mode of operation of any machine tool can be altered; the simplicity of the alteration means that control techniques are applicable to small batch sizes. However, a substantial amount of planning is required to prepare the input tapes and it is sometimes advantageous to enlist the aid of a computer if the preparation of tapes is complicated or time-consuming.

Because control tapes are prepared in advance, there is a tendency to 'play safe' and to program a machine tool for the worst conditions it is likely to encounter; of

6 Numerically controlled machine tool

course, this inevitably means that numerically controlled machine tools are programmed conservatively and that the full advantages of numerical control are not being gained. One method of overcoming this conservatism is to employ adaptive control whereby, ideally, a machine tool is able to adjust its speeds and feeds by employing current tool force, tool wear, or torque readings to adjust existing machining conditions as appropriate. The present difficulty is to obtain reliable and accurate measurements of machining factors, say tool wear, under cutting conditions, and a great deal of research effort is being directed towards the investigation and development of suitable transducers. It is likely that in the short term adaptive control will develop along the lines of in-process or post-process control where the dimensions of workpieces are checked during or after machining and the information is used to correct any tendency of the machine to drift outside known tolerance limits. Another simple, applicable, and worthwhile method of adaptive control is to reduce the time which a machine tool spends 'cutting air', by increasing speeds when the power to the machine drops to a very low level.

Normally a special-purpose computer accompanies every numerically controlled machine tool, its function being to convert the data on the input tape into a form which is consistent with the particular control system of that machine tool. Special-purpose computers are cheaper than general computers but are not so flexible and can usually be used on machine-tool set-up only; however, cost differences between special-purpose and general computers are diminishing, and there is now a trend to employ general computers where possible.

Although numerical control of machine tools increases metal-cutting times, there is a growing realization among machine-tool manufacturers and machine-tool users that there is more to be gained by improving work-handling techniques and by reducing set-up times and inter-machining times, than by concentrating upon increasing metal-cutting rates. The correctness of this type of thinking is verified by the results shown in Table 1, and has led to the manufacturing-unit concept, which can be composed of a number of simple machining operations in a planned sequence to give maximum throughput of work. There are different approaches to layouts of manufacturing unts: sometimes they are arranged to suit the sequence of machining operations, and sometimes to suit the shape and size of workpieces; the latter technique is known as group technology, and is used to a greater extent than the former.

Transfer lines are good examples of the manufacturing unit concept and are capable of maintaining large production throughputs, but they usually contain lines of special-purpose machine tools and, as such, are relatively inflexible in operation.

Machining centres are manufacturing units which have been developed from the philosophy that it is difficult to transfer between and to reset workpieces accurately upon machine tools, and that it is preferable to bring the correct cutting tool to a workpiece as required without disturbing the location of the workpiece. An example of a machining centre is given in Fig. 7. Machining centres are expensive and are sometimes difficult to justify economically, but they do possess the decided virtue that because they are tape-controlled they have a considerable degree of flexibility. Consequently machining centres are accepted in production layouts, and have initiated considerable alterations to workshop arrangements; furthermore, by including a machining centre into the line, transfer lines can be made much more adaptable.

The manufacturing unit concept has developed rapidly during the last couple of years, and perhaps it would be better to use the term integrated manufacturing system to describe the present state of development. The integrated manufacturing system is usually built from a number of machining centres and/or a number of simple machining processes, the system being directly controlled by a large computer, as illustrated

7 Machining centre

in Fig. 8; it is relevant to note that machining costs can be reduced between five and ten times, and that the American Machine Tool Exhibition held recently in Chicago showed emphatically that machine-tool manufacturers have invested heavily in integrated manufacturing systems. The computer directs the work from machine to machine in an efficient manner, and it is imperative that accurate work-handling and location procedures are available. In future, it should be possible to build machining processes, machining centres, and integrated manufacturing systems on a building-block basis as required; the existing trends towards modular construction will assist this development.

Machine-tool manufactuers are well aware that more rapid and accurate control is necessary for work handling, loading and off-loading of workpieces, work transfer, inspection, and assembly procedures to reduce production times still further; again this philosophy is backed up by the results of Table 1; consequently research and development effort is being increasingly directed towards these areas.

It is pointless having efficient machining units, work-handling techniques, etc. if the whole manufacturing area is allowed to become submerged in swarf. Swarf-removal systems must be accepted as essential features of integrated manufacturing systems. Because of likely legislation against the uncontrolled discharge of effluents from factories, steps are already being taken to include swarf-removal systems into manufacturing systems as a matter of course. Swarf-removal systems are also justifiable on an economic basis since reclaimed swarf can normally be sold profitably, and reclaimed cutting fluid can be used repeatedly.

It is more than likely that steady progress will be made in future towards more extensive applications of direct computer-controlled manufacturing systems, and possibly of whole workshops.

NEW PROCESSES

Manufacturers of metal-cutting machine tools are not relying entirely upon better design procedures, more control, and better machine-tool utilization to increase their share of the machine-tool market; they are also improving traditional machining processes and developing new processes.

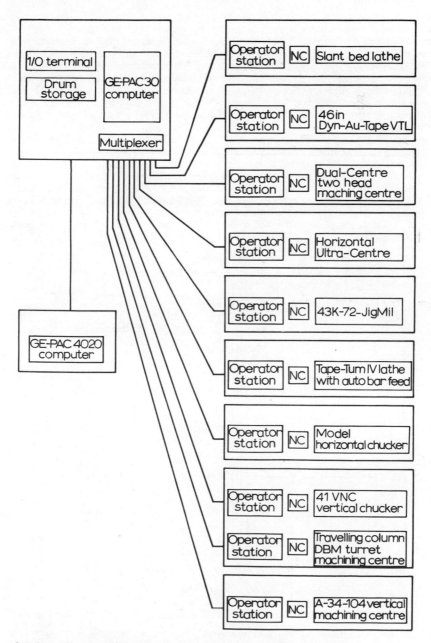

8 Schematic of machine tools directly controlled by computer

It is not possible within the confines of the present text to discuss the developments in each area of machining, and perhaps grinding will be accepted as a reasonable guide to the whole machining field. Until the beginning of the sixties grinding was looked upon largely as a finishing process, although there were obvious exceptions, for example vertical-spindle grinding, slab and billet grinding, etc. However, grinding is now recognized as being capable of economically removing metal at rates which are equal and sometimes superior to those associated with planing, milling, and turning machines; an indication of the present attitude is that the rapid removal of stock by grinding is now referred to as abrasive machining. The application of abrasive machining has largely resulted from the recognition that grinding wheels were underworked in the past and that they are capable of accepting large values of horsepower. The transmission of large powers to grinding regions has been achieved by taking heavier cuts and allowing grinding forces to rise, or by increasing wheel grinding speeds while maintaining conventional grinding forces; of course both methods can be, and have been, carried out concurrently. An indication of the employment of high wheel speed to increase the metal-removal rates associated with grinding is given in Fig. 5; it is worth noting here that abrasive belt machines can maintain substantial rates of metal removal, a figure of 6 in^3 min^{-1}/in width of belt often being quoted for these machines.

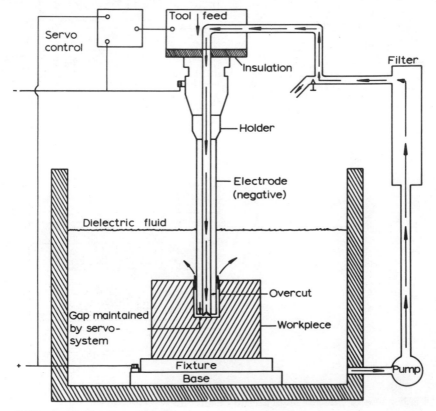

9 Electrodischarge machining

Electrodischarge machining and electrochemical maching are probably the best known of the newer processes, as they have obtained small but significant shares of the market. The two processes are similar in that they are both independent of the hardness and toughness of any workpiece material; also both are used for the manufacture of dies. Electrodischarge machining, which is a recognized toolroom process and which is shown diagrammatically in Fig. 9, utilizes electrodes as cutting tools, electrodes being easy to design but having rapid rates of wear; conversely, electrochemical machining, illustrated in Fig. 10, requires tools which are very difficult to design but which have indefinite lives; the design procedures associated with tools for electrochemical machines are so complicated that computer-aided design methods are necessary, and relevant programs are available at MTIRA. Electrochemical machining has been only slowly accepted by users, the main reasons being that large amounts of workshop floor area are required to accomodate storage tanks for electrolyte, and that initial costs are high; e.g. a machine which can remove metal at a rate of 1 in^3 min^{-1} costs about £35 000. Electrochemical machining has the advantage that it does not leave burrs on machined workpieces; furthermore, its application is not limited to hard materials, since it can readily machine conventional materials.

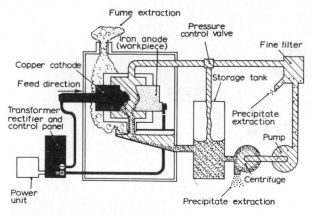

10 Electrochemical machining

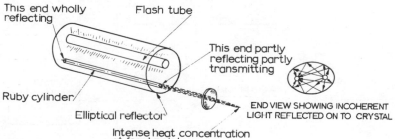

11 Laser machining

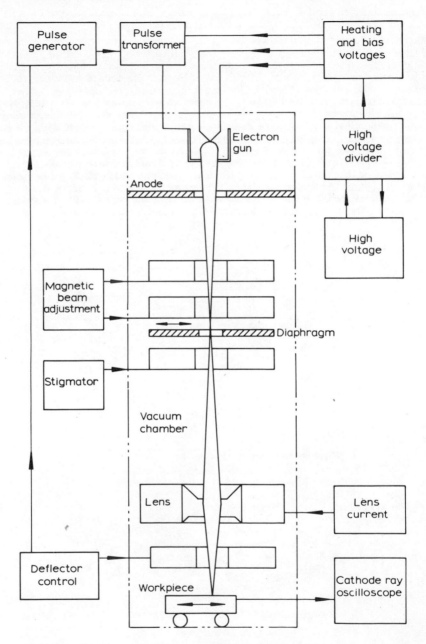

12 Electron-beam machining

Laser machining is another relatively new technique; its principle of operation is shown schematically in Fig. 11. It is normally restricted to cutting sheet metal, but is similar to electrodischarge machining and electrochemical machining in that it is independent of the toughness or hardness of any workpiece material. The bulk of a laser machine is often a disadvantage, and until recently the efficiency of the technique was poor; however, CO_2 molecular gas lasers are efficient and can convert 20% of electrical input energy into machining power. It is anticipated that laser machines will be employed more extensively in the future.

Electron-beam machining focuses an electron beam on to a workpiece (Fig. 12) and evaporates metal locally. It has a similar work range to laser machining, but has the practical disadvantage of requiring a vacuum chamber. Electron-beam welding can weld materials with little distortion, as shown in Fig. 13; it is capable of welding a large range of materials and is expected to increase in popularity, particularly in view of the anticipated future move towards composite materials, and the formation of workpieces by joining techniques.

argon
arc

electron
beam

13 Electron-beam welding with little distortion

A variety of other new machining processes are being pursued at various rates. For example, ultrasonic machining, where abrasive particles are vibrated against a work surface at ultrasonic frequencies to remove metal. Another new technique is high-pressure jet machining, where metal is removed by blasting a high-pressure liquid jet at a work surface.

CONCLUSIONS

Metal-cutting machines are being designed, manufactured, and employed to meet present challenges, and the industry is well placed to accommodate future requirements.

Perhaps the most important aspect is that both metal-cutting machine-tool manufacturers and machine-tool users are aware of future requirements, and are exploring

all avenues to increase production, reduce material wastage, and reduce manufacturing costs, while taking into account the increasing scarcity of skilled machine-tool
operators and the growing divergence of materials which require machining.

REFERENCES

1   M. E. Merchant: *Annalen CIRP,***18,** 1

2   G. Barrow, and F. Koenigsberger: *Machinery,***117,** 9 Sep, 1970

3   'The metal-cutting tool industry 1965-1969, ' US Dept. of Commerce, Business and
     Defense Services Administration, Aug, 1970

4   'The utilization of machine tools', MTIRA, Research Rep. 23, Apr, 1968

DISCUSSION OF THE SECOND SESSION

In the Chair: Professor S. A. Tobias (Birmingham University)

Mr J. D. Harper (John Harper and Co. Ltd): I have two questions for Mr Horton. One point he seemed to me to have omitted at the very beginning, talking about the potential advantages of a casting process, is the possibility of forming internal shapes of some complexity. In most of the papers we have heard this morning this is either impossible, or possible with great difficulty. Mr Horton did not mention it. I wonder whether there is any specific reason for that.

My second point is in connexion with his use of tolerances. He stated a number of dimensional tolerances, giving the impression that one tolerance goes with one process. My experience is not with steel castings but with iron castings: high-duty iron castings of different types; and certainly in that field the tolerance is very much less a function of the process than of the component design. There are many castings where shell moulding will produce a much less accurate casting than conventional sand moulding, due to the relative rigidity of the shell, for example. There are other cases where the casting process is relatively unimportant due to dimensional changes which could occur in heat treatment or fettling operations. Even within a process, the effect of tolerances which could occur across a mould joint, between a mould and a core, and, depending on the metal, many other features of the design, is much more important than the process which is selected. It is important to emphasise this because frequently one sees written on drawings and designs: 'shell moulding', or some other casting process, giving the impression that the draughtsman thinks that in writing that he can guarantee 0·005/in, 0·0001/in, or whatever it may be. This is a dangerous assumption, which is in fact made. The choice of the process depends on very much more than just looking up a table of tolerances.

Mr Horton: I am glad you raised the first point on coring; it was a point which came to my mind which has perhaps not been developed in the paper. The only excuse we can make is that we have perhaps taken it as read that one of the advantages of close tolerances of these processes is on awkward profiles which includes coring.

With regard to your second point on dimensional accuracy, perhaps in my introduction to the paper I developed a little too much on specific tolerances per casting. You have raised a most important point. It does happen quite often that drawings sent in to us for quoting, specify investment castings, meaning shell mould castings, or vice versa. What we have tried to develop in the paper is that each casting is treated on its merits. It depends on volume, configuration and overall size. The process enters into it, but the first consideration is the actual configuration of the component.

Mr V. Kondic (Birmingham University): I came to this conference because of its title, but as the morning wore on, I began to wonder if I had come to the wrong conference. We have heard a great deal about the methods of forming, but precious little about the competitive nature of these methods. This is particularly true of the casting processes paper. Having read the paper, and listened to Mr Horton, one would conclude that either the casting processes are not competitive or the foundries are shy of competition. I am fairly sure that both of these conclusions would be wrong. I have two questions for Mr Horton which I hope will put him in a more competitive frame of mind. Could he tell us under what set of production conditions the casting processes he mentioned are competitive amongst themselves? By 'competitive', I mean competing in engineering terms, metallurgical quality terms, and cost terms.

Second, I am a sort of foundryman myself, and am a little scared that Mr Horton and I may be out of business before long if all these new forming processes come into full production. Can he state to what extent and when, the casting processes he described are competitive with the forming processes we have heard about this morning?

Mr Horton: The first question is the $64 000 question: how is the process or technique described competitive? If I may refer to the major part of the paper, which is on shell moulding, we generally run between 50 and 100 moulds per machine run. Add to this the cost of patterns, which can be from £500—£1 000, then one has to start going into fairly close examination with the customer as to what advantages the casting is giving. What we have tried to show is that the so-called precision casting in isolation is possibly not competitive when compared with other forming techniques, or indeed so-called traditional techniques. What does matter is that the casting is giving overall cost saving. I cannot really think of any way in which I could answer the question without going into a lot of detail, which I think would take a long time, and be outside the scope of this session. What we think we offer as a foundry industry, if I could encompass it in that way, on shell moulding and lost-wax castings in particular, is the multiplicity of castings specifications which can be made, some of which are difficult to forge; add to that the advantages of close tolerances, then one is competitive against the other metal forming techniques.

My answer to the second part of the question is: competition, yes. However, I think that development of foundry processes is accelerating and will continue to accelerate, and that unit costs will come down even further. One of the techniques outlined in the paper was the high-pressure or medium-pressure squeeze unit, which within the author's group of foundries has been installed on a fully integrated layout. Simulated production programes were done by a computer on simulation runs. It is fully mechanized, and I think this is the sort of advance which will keep the foundry industry competitive for a long time.

Mr Brammer: I think, in answer to your question, that basically the terms of reference were not quite specific from the cost aspect of these various processes, and the paper is quite short, as a result of the subject matter to be covered in one day. I feel that the competitive nature of the various processes will be discussed in the third session, for which this is intended. It is obvious that in many directions steel castings are quite competitive. We are in business, and in business to a large extent.

The main point I should like to emphasise is that much more can be done to provide a fundamental link, at the design stage, between founder and designer. The basic difficulty, and I hope that I am not treading too much on designers' toes, is this: do they in fact design with a specific process in mind, or do they design a component, and then jockey it about to where they can get it best produced? The application of value analysis techniques to the unit cost of components has clearly demonstrated that there is still a large market where steel castings can compete with other processes in terms of the least unit cost of finished component.

Mr W. Beattie (Lamberton and Co. Ltd): Mr Thomas asked us to be controversial, and I would like to take him up on that and do a bit of rabble-rousing. I refer to Figs. 8 and 9, where there is a diagram showing percentage strain on two types of presses.

These appear like Daily Express opinion polls. The rate of strain is a function of the stress, and the stress is a function of the area of the component. The cranks are bending as a function of the diameter. Therefore all these terms of strain are purely parameters which the designer can influence. In other words, these two graphs can be made to look identical.

Mr Thomas: In preparing the paper on such a wide field, I have gone into areas where I am by no means as expert as the questioner. Certain of these figures are taken from another author and I chose to leave out the figures with the double pitman in. These bring the conventional presses closer to the wedge presses. I think that so much of the question of strain is a function of the design of the machine, and that necessarily the wedge press has probably been made stiffer. I accept that there is no fundamental reason why we should not make a conventional press stiffer.

On the table loading, I think you would accept that with a conventional press with a single throw you run into trouble if you forge very far off centre. This is to some extent overcome by using a double throw shaft, but because of the guiding system, which we will call a wedge, this is purely and simply another means of achieving this.

Dr Farmer: I would like to raise two points: first would the authors like to comment on the viability of automatically die casting steel components in permanent moulds; and second, have the authors done any work on producing castings by immersing the mould in molten metal rather than pouring metal into a mould?

Mr Horton: We do cast some die steels. We went into a fairly lengthy development with a customer using cast die steels for forging dies, and the outcome of the exercise was that we looked as though we were going to put a considerable number of diesinkers out of a job, and the work ceased at that point. It is an awful thought, but this is partly what we are up against as a nation, I suppose. Yes, we do die steels, but they are not easy to handle in some respects from a casting point of view.

Mr C. G. Glen (Yorkshire Imperial Metals Ltd): I would like to follow up what Dr. Farmer tried to get going. What cost saving could we expect if the Shaw process was used to make forging dies? What are the cost savings compared with machining out of bought stock?

Mr Horton: I cannot answer that question. It is very complex because we would have to know the customers' total machining costs. All I know is that as we understand it we finished up with a complaint by the Die Sinkers' Union, and the job stopped at that point.

Mr J. E. Russell (BSC Special Steels Division): Mr Thomas referred to the Auto Forge process which looked very promising. However, although the workpiece is cast into a die, it is removed after solidification and transferred to a forging station. Could Mr Thomas say what happened to a process (which we used to term 'slush forging') that was the subject of much discussion three or four years ago, whereby liquid metal was cast into the bottom die of a forging machine and then, after a short time when the liquid had partly solidified into a slushy state, a top die was brought down? The die-movement could be fast or slow depending on how much spread had to be given to the material. As solidification was completed very rapidly and under high pressure, the structure was very fine. This process seemed to be ideal for the alloys that were very difficult to forge by conventional means, like the more exotic nickel-based ones.

Mr Thomas: To the best of my knowledge, it never got beyond the Iron Curtain as a serious attempt at a production process. Most of the work I have seen reported on emanates from Russia. There was probably a lesser interest in America, but the suggestions in the Russian literature were that there were at least pilot plants working. However, I have never heard of any real attempts to make the process work in the Western World.

SELECTION OF PROCESSES FOR THE MANUFACTURE OF SMALL COMPONENTS

R. L. Sands

Selecting a process for the manufacture of many types of component often turns out to be a fairly simple and straightforward task. It is done many times every day, in many different ways, and by people having widely differing expertise and objectives. In some cases it will be the component designer who is responsible for the selection; in other cases a buyer or a production engineer will make the decision; and, fairly often, it is the producer who decides.

The authority for making the decision as to which process will be used varies from company to company, and within one company it may change with the circumstances. If the component is of a type which is new to the purchaser, and there is a large technical content implied by the specification, then the designer is likely to be the person most concerned with process selection decisions. For components which are technically simple, and also for those parts which are difficult, yet essentially similar to others already being purchased, then a buyer may be able to make all decisions which determine the type of process to be used. Where several processes are involved in the manufacture of the component a production engineer should play the dominant rôle. It is important to note that there is often a distinction to be made between the person who has authority to sanction the use of a method of manufacturing and those most concerned with securing the benefits of optimum process selection.

Related to the question of who selects the process is the equally complex problem of how the merits of the competing processes are judged. The problem is usually summarized by saying that the aim of the purchaser is to achieve minimum cost coupled with acceptable quality. The critical factor here is to define the acceptable quality. Assuming that there is a direct relationship between process costs and quality, almost by definition minimum cost cannot be achieved unless the minimum acceptable standard has been established. Quality standards are not themselves difficult to set, but to define the boundary between what is acceptable both sofar as short-term performance of the component is concerned and for maintaining the long-term company image, is much more difficult.

This paper examines some problems which may be encountered when selecting the optimum process for the manufacture of small components which are required in relatively large quantities. One of the difficulties is the wide range of circumstances in which decisions determining process selection may be taken. The features of a component design are shown to exert a large influence on the choice of process. Since the producer is likely to have a much more extensive knowledge of his process than the component designer, close cooperation at the design stage between user and manufacture is essential if the desired combination of minimum price and acceptable quality are to be achieved. Various cost determining factors are considered, and the importance of relating the primary production process to later operations, such as machining, is noted. The ways in which material costs and production quantity also influence process selection are illustrated.

The author is with the Metal Components Division of BSA

621.91:
65.015

A rather different type of problem is met when the implications of the quantities to be produced are considered. As quantities increase more economical manufacture is expected. This is achieved both by the economies of scale which can accrue with the operation of any process but also with the possibility of gaining cost savings by changing from one process to another. The concept of there being a minimum order quantity, which is an important feature of all manufacturing processes, is well known. It is known that the concept arises out of need for special purpose tooling and high setting-up costs for certain operations; since these operations and costs are incurred whenever the process is used it is assumed that the minimum order quantity is a constant for the process. However, consider Fig.1, which shows the quantity/cost relationships for two hypothetical processes which are competing for the production of a component. Somewhere in the region of a 15 000 production quantity there is a point above which it is more economical to produce by process A. From such relationships the magnitude of the minimum order quantity is established. What is frequently not appreciated is that the order quantity at which A becomes viable is a function of the cost charcteristics of the competing process B as well as those of A. Thus the value of the minimum order quantity is not an invariant, but depends to some extent upon the alternative methods of manufacture which are available.

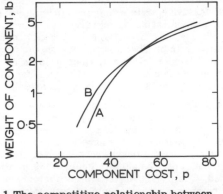

1 **The competitive relationship between two processes**

It is hoped that, by outlining some of the problems, the nature and extent of the difficulties in treating process selection as a logical and systematic activity has been shown. The difficulties arise not only from the widely differing circumstances in which selection is made, but also because personal judgement, rather than formal rules, plays a dominant part in the decision

For several reasons the detailed consideration of the specific merits of the various available processes has not been adopted in this paper as a means of considering process selection Firstly manufacturing technology has become so complex and specialized that it is not possible within the compass of a short paper to adequately examine the critical features of a large number of processes. Secondly, it must be recognized that while several of the most important basic processes for the production of small components have been widely used for very many years: drop forging, investment casting, deep drawing, etc., important modifications and combinations of processes are constantly reaching commercial fruition. Examples of this are fine-blanking, sinter-forging, press-casting, etc., and for these, especially the hybrid processes, there is not yet sufficient experience of the range of application to determine how they will alter the previously established competitive balance between processes. Since this dynamic situation will always be an important feature of process technology, it seems more important to examine the underlying principles of selection which are likely to be somewhat more permanent. Finally, the technical features of several of the important processes have been considered in the papers presented earlier and little would be gained by their repetition.

This paper therefore treats the problem of optimum process selection for small components required in large quantities in a rather broad manner, and highlights some of the more important of the factors encountered.

COMPONENT CHARACTERISTICS

Each manufacturing process can be viewed as having a characteristic combination of cost, and product type. Thus for each process there are certain shapes, accuracies, materials, properties, finishes, etc. which are characteristic of the method. Combined with this is a characteristic range of manufacturing costs. The significance of this 'combination of characteristics' is that it defines the limits for economic/competitive production, i.e. it is based upon practical experience of operating the process in competition with other manufacturing methods. The 'characteristics combination' defines the range of products for which the process has been able to successfully compete.

The important technical factors which determine process selection seem to be: shape/form and specific design features, dimensional accuracy/surface finish and properties/materials. When the influence of these upon the choice of manufacturing process is analysed it is found that as any factor is taken towards its technical limit, the number of possible manufacturing processes is reduced. Obvious examples of this are the need to make certain extremely complex shapes by investment casting, the production of certain steel components requiring exceptionally high properties from forgings, and the need to make specific types of self-lubricating bearings by powder metallurgy methods.

This general rule which states that as the determining parameters approach their extreme values then so does the number of suitable production routes become more restricted, has important corollaries. For instance, as one parameter approaches its extreme value, then for a given manufacturing method the permissible range for the remaining parameters is correspondingly reduced. Also, if more than one parameter must approach extreme values, then a single manufacturing method tends to become inadequate and it becomes necessary to adopt multiple operation processing. An example of the latter circumstance is the production of gears for a high duty transmission application; these need to combine a high level of properties with a high degree of precision; to achieve this will require forging as the primary process, and machining to achieve the accuracy.

The use of multiple process operations in which the final shaping operation is machining, is so widespread that it is paradoxically sometimes ignored. Indeed it is sometimes linked with activities such as transport, and regarded as having little bearing on process selection. There are many cases where components are commonly referred to as being 'forged' or 'cast' when from the point of view of describing their processing it would be more correct to say that they are machined. This point is made because of its relevance to a proper appreciation of component production costs. Consider the case of a component which has cost £0·6 to produce. Of this, £0·45 is the machining cost and £0·15 the cost of the forging; if one is looking for an improved process in order to achieve significant cost reduction then it is the £0·45 machining which is likely to be the key.

SELECTING A PROCESS

I have pointed out that for each process there is a characteristic combination of features such as shape, size, tolerance, material, surface finish, properties, etc. which characterize the method. Furthermore, for each established process this combination of characteristics has been proved to be competitive in terms of price and quality. A consequence of the existence of these characteristics is that it is often fairly easy to examine a component drawing, and by noting the various design features and material specification to be able to identify immediately the optimum method of manufacture. A superficial interpretation of this is that in a large number of cases the selection of the optimum process is by no means difficult. On must, however, beware of confusing the fully detailed component design with the less easily grasped concept of the component function.

When a component is designed it is given details which are related not only to its function but also to some envisaged method of manufacture. That is, the designer will have in mind a method of production and he will modify his basic functional concept in order to meet known production requirements. In doing this the designer must, by virtue of his responsibilities, choose a process which his experience indicates will be capable of producing the desired component and give an acceptable quality.

Thus when a drawing is examined and the component is seen to be suitable for only one method of manufacture, this is really a reflection of the designers skill and does not imply that alternative methods of production cannot offer advantages. Almost always when components are required in large quantities, alternative production routes should be considered, although this may only be of value when significant design concessions are permissible.

Consideration of the component shown on the right in Fig. 2 may help to make clear this relationship between design concessions and process selection. If, for some reason, the form shown could not be changed without detriment to the function of the part, then economical manufacturing is probably restricted to the method envisaged by the designer, namely the assembly of a number of machined and blanked parts.

In some cases the design concessions needed to make an alternative process feasible are minor ones. For a casting process perhaps only the inclusion of corner or root radii or the relaxation of tolerance across one face. However, once the principle of some design concessions being acceptable is established then this should be taken to its logical conclusion and the acceptability of the changes necessary to accommodate lower cost processes should be examined. For the component shown on the right in Fig. 2 the ultimate solution was to manufacture by a powder metallurgy method the part shown on the left.

In the example used it is quite clear that by studying the function of the component in relation to a low cost production route it has been possible to achieve very large cost savings. It must be emphasised that these have been achieved without any sacrifice in performance. Indeed when one is able to replace an assembly of parts by a single precision component it is not unreasonable to expect an improved performance as well as reduced costs. Thus the design concessions required are concessions of form, not of quality.

2 Component made by assembling several parts, and the single precision
powder-metal part which replaced it, shown on the left

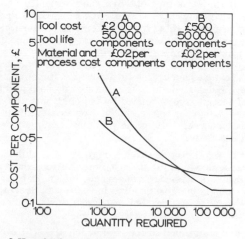

3 How high raw-material costs limit the
size range over which a process is
competitive

The conclusions to be drawn from this analysis are sufficiently important to be re-stated, hence, the detailed design of a component is not determined by function alone, optimum process selection almost always requires some changes to the initial design, and design concessions do not necessarily imply a lowering of quality standards.

To take this consideration of design concessions a stage further it is instructive to try and subdivide the various features of a design into categories according to their role. For instance:

(i) the most obvious type of feature is the general shape. Shape can be considered sofar as process selection is concerned, as being a first 'sorting' criteria. Thus components with a large plan area but small thickness are likely to be best produced by one of the sheet forming processes; axisymmetrical components with large length to cross-section ratios are probably going to be made by an extrusion operation; hollow components with complex internal forms will probably have to be cast, etc. Shape alone does not usually determine which is the best process to use, at least not in detail, but it does enable a large number of unsuitable processes to be eliminated from consideration

(ii) a further feature-type are the design details essential to the functioning of the component. In this category are included the modifications to the basic form, the tolerances, material or property specification, surface finish and special features such as screw threads etc.

(iii) another type of design feature are those related to the production process rather than to the components function. These include draft angles, machining allowances, corner radii, location points etc. The precise nature of this type of feature is obviously related to the manufacturing method, and if this is changed so must many of the features in this category

(iv) there may also be a further category of features having a similar rôle to those of Type 3, but which are related to the needs of an individual producer. Although several producers may operate the same general process and be in competition with each other for the same type of work, their capabilities will vary in small, but nevertheless significant ways. Difference in plant, tooling practice and experience can give rise to this type of difference between producers. Again, if the aim is to get the best possible combination of price and quality, account must be taken of these individual idiosyncrasies.

By classifying design features according to their rôle, it can be seen that to choose the optimum process, the design details are dictated by both purchaser and producer. The first two types of feature are specified by the designer, who may also be able to specify most of the third group for traditional processes. It is likely, however, that in many cases the producer will be the principal authority determining these as well as the fourth type of feature.

Although perhaps not as explicitly as producers may wish, this dual designer/producer approach is widely recognized. In practice it is the third group of features which may cause trouble. Sofar as these are concerned, designers often believe that their previous experience enables them to provide in the initial design all of the features required for successful manufacture. But of necessity a designer bases his approach on experience and this must lie in the past.

With new processes, and traditional processes which are still evolving sofar as technical details are concerned, the subtle details which determine optimum processing are continually changing. These details are normally meaningful for reducing costs and improving quality only when they have emerged from commercial manufacturing experience. Therefore it is natural for there to be a time gap between when manufacturers acquire a body of 'know-how' which enables some form of improvement to be achieved and the communication of the details of this to users. As well as the time gap there is also likely to be a comprehensive gap between the producer, who needs to master all aspects of his process, and the user's designer who needs, or can assimilate, much less detail. The existence of these gaps does not necessarily imply secrecy or non-cooperation on the part of the manufacturer, it is often a reflection of the difficulty in systemising such knowledge and relating it to other 'know-how'.

The implications of this situation are clearly that no matter how skilled is a designer, the producer can almost always find ways of reducing manufacturing costs if he is allowed design concessions.

COST-DETERMINING FACTORS

Earlier in this paper the usual statement of the overall objective for process selection was given as being to obtain components at the lowest cost consistent with acceptable quality. In this section of the paper it is intended to look at some aspects of how process costs are determined.

There is often a very great preoccupation with the costs due to the labour content of the processing. While labour costs are important it is usually as well to distrust statements such as: 'it's a very good process but can't compete because of the amount of manual work involved'. Except for processes which have only just reached an intermediate stage in their development such statements almost always avoid the real issues. Generally, if a method of component manufacture can offer some important cost advantage (use of cheap raw materials, efficient utilization of consumable materials, produce components with sufficient accuracy to eliminate a machining operation, etc) then ways will be found to mechanize or automate the process, and thereby drastically reduce labour costs. For an established process inability to compete due to large labour content is therefore likely to cloak some more fundamental reason which has been responsible for making uneconomic the capital investment which would have enabled the labour content to be reduced.

Other important aspects of cost determination emerge from the relationship between production quantity and unit cost. Some processes are characterized by being capable of producing a very low cost only when very large quantities are involved. The origin of the need for large quantities before minimum production price is achieved is the cost of special tools (i.e. the tools which are specific to the production of the particular component) and the cost of setting-up a production run. The latter cost is, of course, as much related to production batch-size as it is to the total order quantity. Naturally the more expensive the tools, the larger the order quantity needed for competitive manufacture.

Tool costs are important in the present context of process selection in ways other than their simple effect upon order quantity. In some processes the tools are subjected to quite arduous conditions. For instance the drop forging, fine blanking, and powder metallurgy processes all make severe demands on the tools used. For other processes, such as shell moulding, investment casting, etc., the tools are not subjected to severe conditions. This distinction is important because if tool costs are high then tool life is a very important factor in determining the viability of the method. Furthermore, tool life itself will, for those processes in the first group in which the tools encounter arduous conditions, be a variable depending upon various factors including the limits to which the manufacturer is prepared to aim. Thus improved accuracy from drop forging probably means reducing the number of components produced between reworking the die; higher density powder metal parts will require a greater compacting load; which means higher tool stresses, and reduces the number of components produced before the tools need replacing.

It must be remembered that the technology of many processes is not so well established that it is always possible to design tools with certainty. The ability to modify tools if they are found unsuitable is therefore an important feature of a process. Processes which do not make great demands upon the tooling clearly have an advantage in this respect, for instance inserts can often be made to modify casting patterns, but for blanking tools even small modifications to profile will probably require a new tool set.

Material costs are another important feature to be considered in process selection. Metallurgists are familiar with the cost penalty of using highly alloyed steels, and research into improving the properties of low alloy steels has been important in minimizing component costs. There are, however, other aspects to material costs which are also important. The advantages of forming components direct from the melting stage have often been cited as a way of minimizing costs. It should, however, be remembered that melting is itself about ten times as expensive in energy costs as is deformation, and is only likely to give a cost advantage if it enables low cost materials to be used, e.g. the scrap from another process; or if by recycling process scrap, the efficiency of material usage is greatly improved.

If a particular process requires the use of relatively expensive raw materials then obviously it will need to offer other substantial advantages in order to justify it use. Also it is likely that the competitive balance between processes using raw materials of different cost will change with component size. An example of this is shown in Fig. 3, where it is supposed that components are required in various sizes, and that they can be produced by drop forging and by powder metallurgy. For the former the raw material costs about 3p/lb while iron powder costs about 4p/lb; the selling price of simple drop forgings is taken as four times the raw material costs and powder costs as one third of the total price. Since the powder metal part is sufficiently accurate to eliminate certain machining operations, the machining costs for the two processes differ, and are taken as 21p for the powder metal part and 28p for the forging. Figure 3 shows that as the weight of the component increases so does powder metallurgy become uncompetitive relative to drop forging.

The rôle of machining costs in determining process is a most important one. The majority of components need to be machined to achieve the required accuracy, and very often the machining costs form the greater part of the manufacturing cost. Thus the accuracy and type of form which can be produced are among the most important factors in determining the use to which a process is put. Perhaps a factor which is not so obvious is the small value of quite large improvements to accuracy. Suppose a part is required which can be produced by two methods, one which gives $0 \cdot 025$ in. accuracy, and the other giving a form which is correct to $0 \cdot 005$ in. The value of the extra accuracy of the second method may or may not be significant depending upon whether it eliminates any machining operation. If the accuracy required is $0 \cdot 003$ in., a tolerance which could perhaps be achieved by a single maching cut from the components produced by either method, then the extra accuracy is virtually valueless; indeed it could be a disadvantage if in trying to produce near-to-finished size to save materials, the machinist is faced with a more costly setting-up operation.

Process accuracy and ability to produce complex forms is therefore only of value if it can eliminate a subsequent operation. Judgement of whether this is possible and how best to take advantage of the possibilities demands a knowledge of both the primary production process; the individual producers' needs; of machining techniques and the equipment available for machining. Naturally this comes back to the critical feature of all process selection: cooperation between producers and users.

ACKNOWLEDGMENT

The permission of the Birmingham Small Arms Co. Ltd to publish this paper is gratefully acknowledged.

FORMING METHODS FOR SPECIFIC FORGED PRODUCTS

R. E. Winch and K. J. Abbott

The concluding paper at a conference on 'Competitive methods of forming' is perhaps a fitting medium through which to emphasize the importance of technical consultation between the buyer and the manufacturer. Such consultation made at an
early stage in design can do much to ensure choice of the optimum manufacturing
process for a component and so achieve a balance between quality and final cost.
For instance, the initial cost of a metal component before machining is not necessarily indicative of the final cost. The designer requires a certain minimum service
at the lowest cost and he must consider size, shape, weight, strength, and appearance,
together with any special features of a particular part.

For many components there can be an obvious choice of basic manufacturing process but this is not always the case, and the purchaser, who cannot hope to have in
his possession all the expertise available to the manufacturer, can in such instances
limit the application of this specialized knowledge. To illustrate this important
factor, and because it would not be practicable to enter into sufficient detail for a
wide range of components, three types of product have been selected for the purpose
of this paper: axle shaft forgings, gear forgings, and universal joint spider forgings.
Since the experience of the authors is limited to the field of forging, it has been
necessary to select examples from this sphere of activity, but we believe that such
examples are indicative of the metal forming processes as a whole.

Brief reference is also made to the types of plant required as an illustration of the
wide range of manufacturing equipment available.

MANUFACTURE OF AXLE SHAFT FORGINGS

A wide range of flanged axle shaft forgings is produced for use in automobiles, commercial vehicles and tractors. They are of the same fundamental design, having a
long stem of relatively small diameter and a thin flange at one end of much larger
diameter. In general, the flange and the stem are formed in two separate manufacturing operations. There are a number of methods of performing both operations,

Selecting the optimum manufacturing process for a particular metal component
should result in a proper balance being established between quality and final cost.
Axle shaft forgings and gear forgings have been chosen to illustrate the wide variations in possible methods of manufacture that can exist, and to show the need for the
closest possible cooperation between buyer and supplier when design and manufacturing methods are under consideration. Instances also occur where existing production methods can be restyled with appreciable benefit. To illustrate this, details
are given of a change in the production method for a universal joint spider which resulted in the manufacture of parts to a higher degree of precision, while a substantial
saving in material was made. Prospective purchasers of formed metal parts should
be prepared, in addition to considering conventional production methods, to realize
fully the implications of both new and improved forming techniques, that they might
purchase the most reliable parts for their purpose at the lowest price.

The authors are with GKN Forgings Ltd.

621.735.04:
65.015

and various combinations of these can be used to produce forged shafts. A description of these processes will illustrate the wide variety of routes which the manufacturer may follow to obtain the forged product.

Methods of forging the flange

There are two basic methods by which the flange can be formed: mechanical upsetting, and electrical upsetting. Friction welding and flash butt welding are considered as further possibilities.

MECHANICAL UPSETTING

Formation of the flange by mechanical upsetting provides a versatile approach in that it permits formation of the flange from stock already preformed to the shaft dimensions. In occasional circumstances the flange can be mechanically upset direct from hot-rolled round stock of the required shaft diameter, but this can only be done when the ratio of the size of the upset flange to the diameter of the shaft is relatively small.

Mechanical upsetting of the flange is performed on a horizontal forging machine which consists essentially of a rigid cast steel body, a stationary and a moving gripper die plate, and a crank to which is attached a header slide. Dies are attached to both gripping die plates and to the header slide. To produce the flange, sufficient steel at the appropriate end of the stem is heated to forging temperature. The stock is placed in the stationary gripper die and the second gripper die is moved to hold it firmly. The header die is moved towards the stock and this forces the heated length of ungripped stock, which protrudes from the grip dies, into cavities in the dies. More than one such operation is necessary to complete the flange, and multiple station die sets are used; Fig. 1 shows a typical horizontal forging machine.

1 Horizontal forging machine

ELECTRICAL UPSETTING

A second method commonly used is to preform the flange of an axle shaft by electrical upsetting, and then finish forge it in a friction screw press. One end of a length of round bar stock is progressively resistance heated and upset into an 'onion shape' by an axial force applied to the opposite end of the bar. While still hot the shaft is then transferred to the friction screw press to complete forging of the flange. The flash is finally clipped from the forging in a separate press.

A general view of plant used in this method of manufacture is shown in Fig. 2. Two semi-automatic electrical upsetters, seen on the left of the illustration, each have a transformer capacity of 80kvA, and an upsetting pressure of 12 tons; movements on these machines are by oil-hydraulic drive. The two upsetters serve heated preformed pieces to the friction screw press seen in the centre of Fig. 2. This press has a nominal working pressure of 800 tons, and a maximum of up to 1 500 tons. An interesting feature of the press is that the bolster secured to the press bed has a swivel action, thereby facilitating handling of the preformed stock into the bottom die, which is fitted to the bolster. After the shaft has been dropped through the bottom die, this die tips backwards into a vertical position. The ram, with the top die fitted, then descends and forges the flange. On the return stroke of the press the die tips forward with the shaft ejected, making for easy removal.

2 Electrical upsetter and friction screw
press installation for forging of axle
shaft flanges

The electrical upsetting method, which permits gathering of extremely long lengths of stock, is the one used most frequently when the axle stem is of the original bar diameter. For this process it is necessary for the bar surface to be smooth enough to slide through the electrodes, and either reeled or ground material is best for this purpose.

WELDING

Some interest has been shown in the manufacture of axle shafts by making the flange as a drop forging and joining it to the shaft either by friction welding or by flash butt welding. Applications for this process could exist where the flange is particularly large in relation to the shaft or is beyond the capacity of the upsetters available. Tests have shown that friction welded shafts have adequate strength and ductility but a limited value analysis exercise has shown that for small shafts, costs are higher, savings on medium shafts are small, and quantities required of larger shafts are often too small to justify the purchase of a machine unless other uses could be found for it. One possible advantage of the process would be to provide shafts having stem and head of dissimilar materials.

Methods of forging the stem

There are three basic methods by which the stem of an axle shaft can be hot formed: by use of the original bar stock; by gap rolling; and by rotary swaging. Stems can also be produced by cold extrusion.

USE OF ORIGINAL BAR STOCK

Where the stem of an axle shaft consists of a plain parallel section, it is possible in some instances to form the flange directly from bar stock of the required stem diameter. This method is dependent on the relative geometry of stem and flange; it can only be used when the diameter of the bar stock is adequate.

GAP ROLLING

Gap rolling provides a particularly versatile way in which to form any stem configuration. In addition to parallel stems, both stepped and tapered stems can be formed. A particular advantage is that square billets, which are cheaper than round material, can be used in this operation which is carried out before the flange is formed.

Gap roll machines are self-contained and portable. They are akin to a small rolling mill except that the rolls are not fully cylindrical in shape. The resultant gap in the rolls permits the operator to feed the heated stock between them. A sequence of passes through profiled grooves in the rolls enables the required stem configuration to be achieved. A typical gap rolling operation is shown in Fig. 3.

3 Typical gap rolling operation

For some shafts formed by gap rolling, particularly those with tapered stems, it is necessary to provide a swelling in the stem at the opposite end to the flange in order to accomodate the spline. In such instances it is normal to finish the stem with a peining operation. This involves rapid hammering of the part while it is rotated between full-length dies on a drop hammer, the residual heat from the rolling operation being used. Peining provides an accurate means of controlling the stem dimensions.

ROTARY SWAGING

The rotary swaging method is one that can also be applied to a wide range of stem configurations. Round stock is commonly used for this type of application, and a peining operation is not necessary.

The basic action of a rotary swaging machine is that small hammer heads acting in concert deliver short rapid blows to the workpiece as it is being rotated and fed through them. Stepped or tapered shafts can be formed.

Advantages of this process are: the machines are easy to set up; tooling is cheap simple and readily maintained; and a product of high quality and accuracy can be achieved consistently with a minimum of technical supervision. Rotary swaging machines are available in the fully automatic form incorporating program control facilities. A vertical rotary swaging machine is illustrated in Fig. 4.

4 Vertical rotary swaging machine

COLD EXTRUSION

Shafts can be produced by cold extrusion, but the flange is still required to be hot-formed by mechanical upsetting as previously described. However, cold extrusion necessitates use of more expensive round steel stock, and this has to be normalized, shot-blasted, phosphated, and soaped before extrusion. A special-purpose hydraulic horizontal press (Fig. 5) can be used for cold extrusion of the stems of axle shafts.

Specific examples

Space does not permit the provision of examples for all of the manufacturing processes already described to produce axle shafts of varying designs, but two examples are given below.

In the first example the following production sequence was selected for the splined axle shaft having a change in diameter along the length of the stem as shown in Fig. 6: this shaft is made from $2\frac{1}{2}$ in square billet, and there are three separate stages of heating and forging.

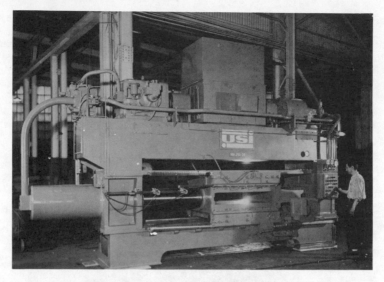

5 Special purpose hydraulic press for cold-extruding axle shafts

The first stage illustrated by the piece on the left of Fig. 6, shows the stem portion of the shaft after being formed in a sequence of gap rolling operations. Next, the length of square stock remaining at one end of the bar from gap rolling is heated and mechanically upset on a large machine to form the flange in four operations including clipping; as shown by the second, third, fourth, and fifth pieces in the illustration. After cutting to length (sixth piece), the small end is heated and mechanically upset, in three operations on a small machine, to form the shape required to accommodate the spline, as shown by the three pieces on the right of Fig. 6.

In the second example, Fig. 7 shows a shaft for a light car; the shaft diameter is constant except for short portions adjacent to the flange. In this instance the head is preformed by electrical upsetting to the shape shown in the upper illustration. The flange and the adjacent collars are then finish-forged in a friction screw press. Finally, the flash is removed from the flange in a clipping press.

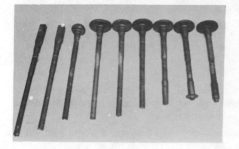

6 Stages in manufacture of commercial vehicle axle shaft

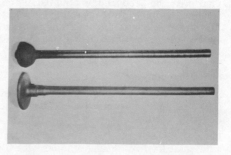

7 Stages in manufacture of light car axle shaft

Variables in axle shaft manufacture

To illustrate the variables involved in arriving at a process sequence in the manufacture of an axle shaft, a broad indication of some of the main influences is given in Table 1.

The wide range of processes available for the production of forged axle shafts and the considerable number of variables that exist make early consultation with the prospective manufacturer essential if the optimum combination of design and manufacturing process is to be realized. It should be noted that all of the methods referred to can be automated, at least to some extent, but that this is not normally economical unless very large production runs are involved.

FORGED GEAR BLANKS

Gear blanks provide another range of typical forged products for which a number of forging processes are available in their manufacture. The shape and size of those gear blanks required in large quantities varies considerably.

The grain flow achieved in forging a gear blank is of particular significance. The material to be forged is placed in the dies on one of its end faces. During forging the grain flow in the original bar or billet stock becomes reorientated in a series of loops which are radially deformed. Such a pattern of grain flow ensures equally high strength in each machined gear tooth, and also reduces the possibility of distortion during heat treatment of gears which have been machined almost to finished size.

By far the largest number of gear blanks made, and particuarly those produced in long manufacturing runs, are made on forging presses. While this situation is likely to continue, it is interesting to note that several significant developments have taken place in this field. A brief description of the principal methods of producing gear blanks follows.

Press-forged gear blanks

Many single gears are characterized by the length being less than the diameter, and by a relatively large bore. The stages of manufacturing such a forging on a press are illustrated in Fig. 8. This example is one of the more simple forms of press forging made in two blows. The square stock material shown on the left of the illustration is heated to forging temperature, and then scale is removed by deforming it between flat dies to the shape of the second piece shown. It is then finished-forged,

8 Stages in manufacture of single gear blank

Table 1 Some factors involved in light axle shaft manufacture illustrated by arbitrary values

	Method A For shaft B For flange	Capital Cost £'000	Labour required (Number at installation)	Die cost £'000	Material cost £/Ton	Rate per hour	Degree of skill Operator	Technician	Are limitations in shape of shaft involved?
A	Manual roll	15	2	1·0	50	120	MED	HIGH	YES
B	Mech. upsetter	100	3	0·5		180	LOW	HIGH	
A	Manual roll Peining hammer	30	4	2·0	50	120	MED	HIGH	NO
B	Mech. upsetter	100	3	0·5		180	LOW	HIGH	
A	Auto roll	30	1	1·0	50	200	LOW	HIGH	YES
B	Auto upsetter	150	1	0·5		300	LOW	HIGH	
A	Auto roll Peining hammer	45	3	2·0	50	200	LOW	HIGH	NO
B	Mech. upsetter	100	3	0·5		180	LOW	HIGH	
A	Rotary swage	50	1	0·2	60	100	LOW	LOW	NO
B	Mech. upsetter	100	3	0·5		180	LOW	HIGH	
A	Bar stock				70				
B	Elec. upsetters Screw press	100	4	0·5		250	LOW	MED	YES

the flash is removed, and the wad punched from the bore, the last two operations being performed on a separate clipping press.

The manufacturing sequence for producing a crown wheel blank on a forging press is shown diagrammatically in Fig. 9. The first operation involves slight upsetting of square steel stock to remove scale and to form a projection on the bottom of the piece concentric with the location carried in the lower tool. This projection provides the means of location in the next operation, which increases the diameter of the part almost to that of the finished forging. In the final operation in the forging press the rim of the forging is made to conform to the required shape, and flash is thrown at the outside diameter. The forging is subsequently pierced and clipped while it is still hot, using a conventional clipping press.

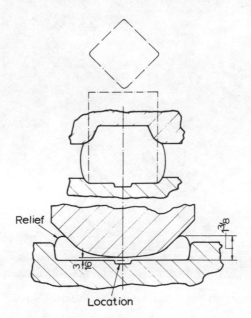

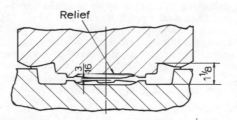

9 Press-forging sequence for crown wheel blank

Automatic forging installation

The need for vast quantities of gear blanks and other circular forgings to a specific pattern, particularly to meet the requirements of the automobile industry, has led to the development of automatic forging equipment. The most significant advance made in the UK in this field has been the introduction of the Garrington 1201 Automatic Forging Installation, the general layout of which is shown in Fig. 10. This plant is capable of producing circular or near-circular components in the weight range 1—6½lb within an approximate diameter range of 2½—4½in. Such forgings have little or no flash and only small draft angles; they are made to close dimensional tolerances. Production speeds achieved are up to 4 200 forgings per hour, nearly ten times the rate typical of a conventional forging press.

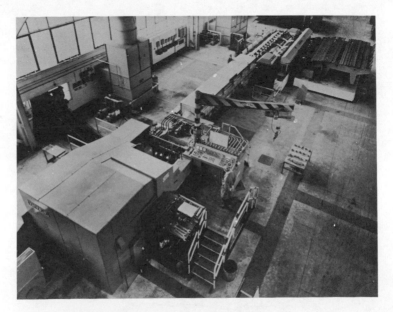

10 Garrington 1201 automatic forging installation

Steel bars 19ft long, delivered in bundles by an overhead crane to a conveyor, are descrambled into a magazine which feeds them into a resistance-type furnace where a full-length bar is heated to forging temperature in less than 1 min. From there they proceed on rollers through a holding furnace which retains the bar at forging heat until ready for acceptance by the forging machine. The bar is sheared, and a sequence of up to four forming operations is performed with all die stations being loaded simultaneously. Fig. 11 shows the sheared steel stock on the left, and the operation sequence for producing a gear-blank forging.

In order to utilize fully the potential of this plant it has been necessary to develop highly specialized die design techniques. The procedure of cutting off a heated piece within the machine permits continuous monitoring of the volume of material being forged. It is this close control over the volume of material in the dies that makes it possible to produce forgings to close dimensional tolerances with little or no flash.

11 Stages in manufacture of gear blank forging on Garrington 1201 installation

Because of the extremely high production rates achieved it is clearly possible to make economic use of such an installation only when suitable forgings are required in very large numbers.

Impact machining

A precision forging technique of particular interest in the manufacture of gears, particularly bevel gears, is that of impact machining. This is now a well established production process, the application of which continues to grow rapidly. Gears made in this way have the teeth formed in the forging operation. On a production basis, tooth form limits are maintained to within 0·0005in, and bevel gear tolerances to BS545 (1949), class C, are consistently maintained. A typical group of impact-machined components is shown in Fig. 12.

Though strikingly simple in concept, the impact-machining process involves the need for precision techniques throughout. A master gear is machined by conventional methods to the requirements of the customer's drawing. This is used to hob a master die which is corrected to a precise form.

In the gear manufacturing process itself, a slug of the required material is first machined to precise limits. This is to ensure both accuracy of form in the finished part and also freedom from such surface imperfections as seams, oxide penetration, and decarburization, all of which may be present in the black bar used. The steel stock is heated in a controlled atmosphere, forged into final shape, and the gear is then cooled in an inert mixture of graphite and sand.

The forging technique used ensures an extremely uniform radial grain flow. As the grain fibre is not cut by tooth machining, both the stress capacity and the load bearing factor of the component are maintained at optimum level. The back face of the gear is subsequently machined and this also removes the forging flash. During this operation the gear is held on the pitch line by a negative tooth form chuck. This ensures a consistently correct relationship between the machined face and the forged teeth. Drilling and fine boring are undertaken as required, the same pitch line chuck being used for the drilling operation. After machining, the gears are pickled and fine shot-blasted, all machining burrs being removed.

Tests have shown that the breaking loads of impact-machined gears are considerably higher than those of gears that have been machine cut. Any forgeable material may be used, including case hardening and alloy steels; bevel gears are currently being produced in En24Z steel.

12 Typical impact-machined components

The size of component that can be produced is limited only by the capacity of available equipment. As a general guide, existing presses cater for components of approximately $3-5\frac{1}{2}$ in diameter.

Use of alloy powder as forging stock

High material utilization makes the use of alloy powder as forging stock particularly attractive in the manufacture of the gear shown on the left of Fig. 13 which illustrates the progress that has been made with this process. A conventional forged gear blank for the same finished part is shown on the right of the illustration. This blank was made from a billet weighing 1160g; the conventional forging weighs 825g, and a finished machined component a mere 300g. The powder metal forging weighs only 382g.

Other advantages of the process are: forging in closed dies eliminates flash; no draught is required; and close dimensional tolerances can be maintained. The forged teeth require only shaving or grinding as a finishing operation.

Work done so far with powder metal forgings has demonstrated that densities higher than 99% are readily obtainable, with mechanical properties comparable to those for the equivalent wrought steel. Future progress in the exploitation of this process is dependent upon the availability, in commercial quantities, of alloy steel powders of similar composition to the wrought steels commonly used.

13 Single gear blank; powder and conventional forgings

RESTUDY OF AN EXISTING PRODUCTION METHOD

So far the paper has been confined to consideration of the production methods available to produce two particular types of forged product in order to illustrate the
wide number of variations in methods that may be available. While the selection of a
correct manufacturing method inevitably arises when considering new patterns, it
should also be remembered that occasions do occur when existing production methods
can be restyled with appreciable benefit. A successful restudy of this kind is described below.

A forged component required in very large numbers in its most popular size is the
spider, or journal, used in automobile universal joint shafts. The choice of forging
process for such a part is clearly most important.

For some years these spiders had been made three at a time using a 1300 ton press
with forging rolls to preform the billet (Fig. 14—right). The method of manufacture
appeared efficient and rapid but, in consultation with the customer (another GKN
company), it was decided nevertheless to explore any possibilities that might lead
to economies.

The outcome of the investigation was the introduction of a new forging method based
on production in singles (Fig. 14—left) using a press of only 500 ton capacity. By
partially mechanizing the operation of this press and the associated trimming press,
a rate of production was achieved almost equal to that of the larger press, and, aris-
ing from manufacture in singles, a number of other economies ensued, as follows:

(i)   the forging was produced to a higher degree of precision. Thus it was possible
      to effect a reduction in machining allowances, and to introduce jig location sur-
      faces in the form of flats on the arms which eliminated a turning operation

(ii) a substantial saving in material was made as the revised method of manufacture
      entailed the formation of very little flash. In fact the volume of steel required
      to make three forgings by the original method was more than sufficient to make
      four by the new method

14 Universal joint spider. Conservation of material with new method of manufacture

(iii) preforming by rolling was no longer required

(iv) the number of operators was reduced from five to three.

It is true that cases of the type described are relatively few. Nevertheless, both the purchase designer and the manufacturer should always be alert to the possibilities of restudying the manufacturing technique when an important parameter in a component is changed.

CONCLUSIONS

If choice of process were a simple matter there would have been no need to hold a conference on 'Competitive Methods of Forming'. The variety of processes available and the complexity of formed metal shapes required from them is such that no individual or group of individuals can provide a simple guide.

It may be asked what benefit can accrue from a description of the various processes available if the contention is correct that hard and fast rules cannot be set down. In the view of the authors it is simply this: the intending purchaser cannot possibly be expected to make an immediate and correct choice in every case; if, however, he can be provided with a wider general knowledge of the available processes in their current forms, he will be better equipped to explore all the possibilities in attempting to achieve his objective of obtaining optimum serviceability at lowest cost.

ACKNOWLEDGMENTS

Acknowledgment is made to the following companies for kindly providing photographs: Lamberton and Co. Ltd, National Machinery Co., USA, USI Clearing Division of US Industries, Inc.

DISCUSSION OF THE THIRD SESSION

In the Chair: Mr B. Carver (GKN Technological Centre)

Mr R. Rajan: During our discussion so far we have not mentioned the problem likely to be created, particularly in foundries and forges, by the availability of labour. The environment in these areas leaves much to be desired since they are generally not only dirty and noisy, but also have a fume-laden atmosphere. Foundries and forges have traditionally drawn their labour from certain geographic areas. Many of the sons and daughters of the traditional work force have educated themselves to a standard which allows them many other means of earning a living. What is suggested will be the movement towards improving the competitive position of the industry, since if it cannot produce the goods it cannot be competitive?

Mr R. M. Gardner (GKN Forgings Ltd)*: So far as the drop forging industry is concerned, I think that Mr Rajan is referring to the traditional hammer forge, since relatively clean conditions prevail in press forges. Semi-mechanization of forging presses represents a first, but substantial, step in reducing labour requirements. Full mechanization comes with the introduction of such equipment as the Garrington 1201 automatic forging installation that was referred to in the last paper. It remains a fact that conditions are not of the best in hammer forges, but I think that steps will be taken to improve this.

Mr Abbot: The points raised by Mr Rajan are certainly germane to the drop forging industry. On the question of noise, much research has been undertaken in attempts to minimize noise from the hammer, but success has only been achieved in reducing the amount of noise emanating from the forge, not the noise level experienced within the forge. I know of many attempts made by managements to persuade operators that they should make use of ear protection that has been provided, but only few have been successful. However, many forges make earplugs freely available and, although this facility is by no means used to the full at present, there is little doubt that this situation will improve with time.

Fumes in the hammer forge are caused firstly by use of lubricants, and secondly from furnaces. Progress in the use of lubricants that are not smoke-forming has been slow but is continuing. So far as furnaces are concerned there is no comparison, in my view, between the 'box of bricks' in common use twenty years ago and the considerably more sophisticated forge furnaces that are used today. Development work on heating techniques is proceeding and it is reasonable to assume that this will result in further improvement to shop conditions.

It must be realized that development of mechanization in the hot metal forming industries has been slower than in those industries where metal is formed cold. The reason for this is both simple and obvious; it is easier to mechanize cold operations than those that are performed hot. Nevertheless, considerable advance has already been achieved in this direction and I anticipate that this kind of progress will continue.

The drop forging industry is well aware that its survival is dependent on a move away from the old ideas of acceptable working conditions.

Mr D. J. Mullet (Acheson Colloids): My company has carried out a lot of work over the past year to lead the field in the production of smokeless lubricants. This was thought to be necessary because of the demand not only of the forging industry, but

---

* **Mr R. M. Gardner** was deputizing for **Mr R. E. Winch**

by other metalworking operations where oil-based lubricants are used which, due to the large amount of fume produced, can be injurious to health and make for unpleasant working conditions. If there is anyone in the metalworking industry who has this smoke problem, don't live with it. Although we cannot as yet replace the use of oil or grease totally, we think that in the light of recent developments at least 75% can be replaced by non-smoking materials.

Mr Abbot: I hasten to assure Mr. Mullett that I had no intention of deprecating the excellent work done by his company. I agree with his remarks in principle, but have yet to be convinced that the percentage quoted is applicable to the drop forging industry.

Mr R. Jenkins (Eva Industries): May I ask Mr. Abbot if he would comment, in relation to the last set of questions, on the remark made at similar meetings elsewhere— that 'the forging industry cannot afford to re-equip on the present job pricing struc-. ture'? Are we going to have to wait twenty years for all noticeable developments, as with the box of bricks, or are we likely to see improvements based on revised economics?

Mr Abbott: Certainly it has been stated in recent months that the drop forging industry must become, in the future, more capitally intensive and less labour and material intensive. Failure of price levels for drop forgings to take into account upward movements in steel prices and wages could only result in a reduction in, or even disappearance of, investment.

If speed of development within the industry is being criticized, then I would offer that section of our paper relating to manufacture of the spider for universal joint shafts, as evidence of the industry's ability to make rapid and significant progress.

May I suggest that the question of whether or not there will be sufficient capital to re-equip is one that should not be put to the forging industry alone. If I read the present financial situation correctly, we have as a nation had to pay so much attention to our balance of payments problems that there is little enough capital available throughout industry for such purposes.

Mr F. Rowley (Perkins Engines Co.): Great emphasis has been made both in this and in earlier sessions on the importance of negotiations between the manufacturer and customer. This is quite right, and I think that in many cases it is the practice. Usually, however, these negotitations do not take place until the designer has committed the method of manufacture and material specification such that only modifications can be applied. If the specialist advice of those involved in all manufacturing methods (e.g. casting, forging, fabrication, etc.) could be applied at the initial design stage, a better and more economic method of forming and choice of material could be possible. Is there any workable solution to this problem? The sort of thing which I have in mind is whether information including working conditions (temperature, stress, etc.), quantities, and dimensions could be fed to a computer which would be programmed to specify the best choice of material and method of forming. If such a scheme was practicable, then the original design drawing would carry full information regarding overall working condition. Only the final working drawing would specify material and method of manufacture chosen so as to achieve the most economic results.

Mr R. L. Sands: I do not see this as a computer problem. It is a communication problem. The latter part of your question regarding materials is very valid. It is particularly true in powder metallurgy, when one often receives drawings marked with something which is useless as regards deciding which material is wanted. You can only go back to the designer and say, 'What do you want it to do? What stresses are involved? What environment is it working in?' He has suggested or indicated the material, not thinking how his product is going to be used. You must look at the function and the conditions under which it will operate.

Mr P. M. Eaton (Unbrako Steel Company Ltd): We are here under the auspices of The Iron and Steel Institute, but I get the impression that most of the people here, and perhaps all the speakers, are production engineers. So here is a steel man saying something, and it is this: do the people who are pushing forward these new frontiers of technology feel that the steel industry in general, and the British steel industry in particular, is giving them the materials they need for these exciting new processes? If not, what is it in particular that they wish they had, and are not getting?

Mr Abbott: It is my view that, in general, the steel industry does a good job, but customers are always critical and constantly seek something better. Mr. Eaton refers to the new frontiers of technology but I would prefer to answer his question by dealing with the present requirements we have of the steelmaker. So far as existing drop forging processes are concerned we are not entirely satisfied with the quality of steel available. We believe that our demands for black bar and billet are in sufficient quantities to warrant some rationalization of roll design so that we may receive a product that conforms more closely to a standard weight per unit length than is the case at present.

The biggest single cause for rejection of steel, or of forgings after they have been made, is for surface defects. We are now obliged to order most of our carbon steel billets to a grading system which specifies maxima for permitted depth of surface defects, and this is not realistic to our needs. Improvements in these directions could not only meet our present requirements but also go a long way towards meeting our needs in the future.

On the subject of hot work steels, we are constantly seeking a die steel that will last longer and will give satisfactory service at higher working temperatures. Improvements in forging techniques that lead to higher production rates only serve to accentuate this need.

These comments are offered entirely in a constructive sense in the belief that British industry, if it is to remain internationally competitive, must strive continually to produce a better end product more economically.

Mr Sands: There is a lot of criticism of die steels made in this country, and many people prefer to buy their tool steels from abroad. I noticed that in Mr. Thornton's paper he specified the use of Swedish tool steel. A lot could be done not only to develop improved materials, but also to make the existing grades more consistent. Consistency is an important problem with many tool steels.

Author Index

---

* discussion page

Subject Index

*discussion page

132

* discussion page